THE
INNOVATOR'S
MINDSET

by Gabriel V. Lechuga

DORRANCE
PUBLISHING CO
EST. 1920
PITTSBURGH, PENNSYLVANIA 15238

Dorrance Publishing Co
585 Alpha Drive
Suite 103
Pittsburgh, PA 15238
Visit our website at *www.dorrancebookstore.com*

ISBN: 978-1-6470-2471-0
eISBN: 978-1-6470-2931-9

INTRODUCTION

As you read this book, you will find that it shares some insider stories, insightful tips, and valuable quotes that will be helpful to any Innovator as they start on their journey to success. To succeed you may want to follow—or maybe not follow—this book, as you may find that after reading it you need more time, and are presently ill prepared to start your very important journey. You may not be ready, according to strategy, logistics, hope, or even in the right mind set. You see, the journey to success can be full of wrong decisions, pitfalls, roadblocks, and dangers that may be lurking around every corner. These may come in different forms, like poor health, failed marriages, a competitor's unsavory sabotage, jealous friends or family members, changing market conditions, etc.

The writer continues to ask this question to those who say that they are seeking for success' sake, and can't wait to start their journey to succeed: Do you really want to succeed? How badly do you want to succeed? How far are you willing to go to succeed? What have you done lately in order to succeed?

Keeping in mind that this book is an innovator's journey, with the motivation to succeed economically, you, the reader, should continue to keep in mind that each individual is different and may seek other goals and/or aspirations. This may come in different forms like wishing for recognition, fame, fortune, and respect, a sense of accomplishment, or even love.

The first and foremost starting goal, or aspiration, in the writer's desire—as he was an innovator himself—was to reach economic prosperity, period! However, as the journey took place and went through its different phases, he began to find out that all of the above-mentioned wishes were interconnected. He started to experience a deeper knowledge and experience from all of these wishes. And in his case, he realized that he had never experienced this deeper sense of interconnected other wishes, or how they would be connected to true happiness or sadness depending on his success or failure.

ECONOMICS

I'm sure that most of us have been through some economic challenges at one time or another during our lives. It's very possible that you may be going through a period of economic challenge at this moment. The reasons for difficult personal economic periods during our lifetimes may be due to a whole host of things that we may not be aware of at the time, and we may very well lack the knowledge or oversight on how they may be affecting us in an economic negative manner. Some humans have said that poverty will always be with us. This is true; however, this is not to be understood as "we will all be poor." It means that poverty will always linger around humanity, but not that we will individually always be economically poor. If you find yourself in an impoverished situation, you may be experiencing feelings of despair, anxiety, depression, shame, and fear for your future and for those that you love, especially your family members. Hey, the writer has been there! This book was written with you in mind. You see, poverty is like a stranglehold that can suck the oxygen and life out of us. It will beat you down and keep you there. Poverty has the potential to act like cancer and can affect communities and eventually even whole countries. This leads to high crime rates, despair, poor health, corruption and a whole host of other malaise. Poverty needs to be eradicated immediately, like a bad disease! However, you must first identify it and plan a course of action, and then eradicate it immediately. Poverty will always fight back and will always be around the corner, so stay vigilant and plan the future. This writer hates poverty and will do whatever it takes to kill it!

So, you may be thinking, "Well, this sounds good and well but how do I get out of this impoverished situation?" Well, you need to build your defenses around you and your loved ones. Fortunately, there are various ways to do this, we will cover these later in the book. Reading this book is a good start on improving your chances to not fall prey to poverty.

The writer witnessed a boy inside a local grocery market asking the grocer for pricing on a small bag of cookies. The grocer responded that the bag of cookies cost $1.99. However, the boy only had $1.75 on him. The boy proceeded to drop his head and walked away. He then asked the grocer for pricing on a small juice drink. The grocer responded that the price was $2.50. Again, the boy hung is head down and walked away. Then for a third time he asked the grocer for pricing on a small bag of candied peanut clusters. The grocer responded, "$1.99." So for one last time the boy hung his head down and walked away—but this time his body language was as if to say, "I give up!"

Yes, poverty and not having the resources to buy what you are in need of can break the spirit and make any human want to give up. The writer has witnessed this up front. However, sad as the story is, it does not end this way. The writer reached into his pocket and offered the boy the balance of the money that he needed. However, he asked that the boy always help others when he grew up, just like he had received help.

Sometimes to escape the debilitating effects of economic poverty, we may need to execute a logistical strategy and escape from poverty's reach. That is why through the long history of humanity, many human beings have decided to migrate, leave their countries of origin and start all over again where there is more opportunity—sometimes even on other continents. In the past, it was about searching for better resources, like more hunting game, more favorable land, a better climate to grow food, etc. In the modern age, it may be about moving to a region that has more economic opportunity and where there are more jobs available, or where there are more businesses to sell to for whatever it is that you are planning to do. While you are strategizing a plan to succeed, the odds must be stacked in your favor. This may not necessarily guarantee your success, but it will improve your chances of succeeding.

It is the writer's opinion that creating a successful business can serve as an economic connector, or link, that can assist us individually to overcome personal challenges—and at the same time, help resolve many of the challenges that modern human society is confronted with, as well as other challenges that may be coming in the future.

We have covered economics, and now we need to discuss how hope can also play a significant role in success. However, as the writer looks back on his journey, there was one thing that he learned, and that is that what matters the most to becoming successful is not just your idea or execution of the plan, but mostly whether you have trust in yourself and in others. Make sure that you have a support group that you can consult with at all times, and that you can confide in and trust. This can come from close friends, but most of the time it comes from family members. This support group will be able to identify any sense or feelings of hesitation or fear on your behalf, and must continue to encourage you to either take the risk or not. Two things will more than likely come over you sometime during your journey: the first one is fear of failure and the second one is that if you fail, you will lose all hope of a better and more secure life for you and your family.

HOPE

Hope is having an aspiration, expectation, goal, or even a dream. Hope can come in many forms and may even be scary because of the fear of failure. You see, having hope is full of challenges, and the desired expectations may not happen. This is a very common human feeling.

Fear in and of itself may create a negative attitude and doubtful feelings, like, "Why try in the first place if I will more than likely fail?" If this is the case, paralyses will surely set in and easily start taking ahold of us and everything around us. We must always be careful about our mindset, what we say, how we say it, and also how we comment about what we think of things. Basically the way we see the world is very important. I always remember during my travels that there are by far many more good people than bad people in the world. This means that the world is an overall wonderful place to live in, and is an environment where success is more likely to be obtained than not. There is always hope to improve our individual situation, no matter what it is. Please never forget that.

If you hope for success and can taste it, you must use the art of visualization. Visualization is something that harnesses the power of the mind and is the power behind every success. Visualization can also become a powerful motivator within itself. In addition to hope, visualization must also be something that you practice to reach your goals of success. We will cover this in more detail later in the book.

This writer is a strong believer in using the power of visualization. A good example of visualization would be like playing golf and visualizing where you would like to hit the ball. This, of course, would be many yards from where your ball is presently standing. Taking the time to visualize the optimal place before striking the ball is necessary; you then address the ball and strike it. Not using visualization will create a random placement of the ball, as you did not choose the ideal spot for the ball to go before you struck it.

However, if you use the art of visualization, it is more likely than not that you will be placing the ball in your ideal spot, or close in proximity. Just like in golf and spotting the ball, you want to make sure that on your way to success, you are as close as possible to landing on your goal. Never play it random! This has much to do with planning and the technique and strategy that you will be using, as well.

STRATEGY

We have already mentioned that every individual has different wishes in life. However, to secure a desired wish, it takes not only having a goal, but also having a plan. Without a plan, it is more than likely that we will never achieve our goals. Plans help to remind us of the goal and how we plan to go about accomplishing it. Planning also helps with upgrading, or evolving, our overall strategy as we are planning our desired accomplishments. Before embarking on your own individual journey, you must plan. You must be well informed, have written reference points, and have access to information that you will need along the way. This is much like preparing for travel, where you pack according to the period of time and according to the terrain that you will be traveling in. You must include all the things that you will need to ensure that your travel goes off without a hitch. Plans must be made in a written format or punch list or they will never materialize, as they'll become impossible to review and otherwise update. Planning takes time and effort—there are no shortcuts! You must never be unprepared when facing the unknown; instead, you must embrace it by being prepared. This will truly make you strong, like forged steel, and even if you don't succeed you will be stronger and better prepared for the next time that you try. Again, when preparing for your journey to success, you must not take shortcuts! Just like a professional athlete trains before a scheduled competition, you must likewise also prepare.

You must also prepare your mindset to be set on the prize, so that no one will be able to throw you off your plan. There may be some ridicule, scoffs and wisecracks from others about you or your desire for success, and it is during these moments that you must always be mentally prepared. It is at this point during your journey that you will find out whether you will have the conviction and stamina to carry your plan forward, so always remember that it's always up to you and only you to succeed! Negativity will always rear its ugly head; however, even when it does, never give up!

Negative to Positive

Sometimes we hear others mention that a bad thing that happened to them was also the best thing that could have happened to them. This means that without the tragic thing, they would have never made a change for the better. The experience of the bad thing that happened to them also serves as a reminder, so that the person does not repeat going through this again. Maybe you're thinking, "I don't need to go through pain or a bad experience to understand what not to do." However, this writer believes that the power of going through a bad experience, or a difficult period, in your life is a good teacher, and the experience serves as a good reference point during your journey to success. You see, when we are faced with a challenge in life, it can serve as a motivator. If we don't adapt, we may become paralyzed and eventually die emotionally, intellectually, or in other ways. This can hardly be called being able to move forward on your journey to success. We will cover this point in detail later on into the book, so that if this becomes something that may trip you up during your journey, you will have the tools to neutralize the challenge and overcome it, showing positive results.

The power of positive thinking has been proven to be an effective dynamic to use when trying to accomplish a difficult feat. The writer believes in this—that you must always try to have a positive outlook during your journey to success. Therefore, this will help you convince others to want to join your efforts, and you will become a more approachable person, therefore making success much more attainable. A positive attitude will help you reach better results along your journey to success. However, this writer does not believe that positive thinking alone will help accomplish your goal. Showing real positive results will take much more than that. The writer is not trying to discourage you from the importance of positive thinking but is trying to re-inforce that this will not be the only thing that will carry you across the finish line of your journey to success. You will need many more tools in your bag to complete the challenge. As a matter of fact, there is an old saying: "Nice guys always finish last." Being nice or positive alone will not carry you to the finish line. Some people can be very competitive, nasty, unforgiving, ruthless, under-handed and many other things, to say the least. These individuals prey on nice or positive individuals; they are bullies that are attracted to them, like hyenas out in the wild attracted to the kill. You must stay clear and vigilant from giving the wrong signals of being overly nice or positive at all times. You must always be fair but firm. This will also be covered later on in the book.

Goals and Dreams

Goals and dreams have been an important part of humanity since the very beginning. Some cultures saw dreams as divine intervention and held them within a great deal of importance. Likewise, you must give dreams and goals a great deal of importance, as they serve as a catalyst for helping control goals or dreams that we may possess at any given time. The energy when chasing a dream will manifest in ways like additional stamina, added energy, willingness to travel much longer distances, being away from home for long periods of time and being willing to go through many other additional sacrifices to reach the goal. When the Spanish explorers of the past were exploring the Americas, there were two primary things that they began looking for. One was eternal youth and the other was great wealth. These were the dreams of a fountain of youth, and the seven golden cities. The Spanish explorers were willing to travel very far to search for their dreams. As humans we all possess different goals and dreams. In the case of one of the Spanish explorers, eternal youth was more important than wealth; however, in the case of the other, wealth was the most important thing. As we discussed before, we all have different dreams and are seeking different things out of life. Therefore, you need to make sure that you are always surrounded by likeminded individuals who possess the same dreams and who are seeking the same goals. This will add more certainty and make your journey to success much more likely to succeed.

If you are constantly having dreams of failure, it may be because you are not happy or are feeling pressure from one thing or another. You may need to simply analyze what is making your subconscious create the dreams of failure and make some adjustments. You may have to think of adjusting who you are surrounded by, or if you are working at a place where you are unhappy and un-comfortable. Or you may not be getting enough sleep and may simply need to go to bed at an earlier time. It can be a whole host of things; however, dreams can be adjusted as your body and mind deem necessary. If your body and mind feel good, rested, and relaxed, it is much more likely that you will have dreams of gaining success. As your dreams become more vivid, you will begin your transformation into becoming more prepared for your journey to success.

LOYALTY

Loyalty is a quality that is not easy to possess and can be very difficult to acquire, especially when our own lives or our own personal interests are at stake. It is quite common to hear that people who face serious criminal charges are willing to testify against their own best friends, family members or even their own spouse. But why? Well, it's because they have the lure of getting rid of all the charges brought against them, to save their own skin. This is called self-preservation, and is common among humans. You might be thinking, "Well, that's a prime example of not having any loyalty!" However, someone else may argue that the end justifies the means. This writer is not going to opine in favor of either argument or the other, and whether the person testifying against others who trusted him or her is loyal or not. After all, we all have to live with our decisions and decide for ourselves whether we lived a moral life or not. In order to succeed, you must also be at peace with whatever actions and decisions you make.

Loyalty is a tool that you will need as you journey on the road to success, for along the way may come some opportunities that could allow you to take a quick profit or to take shortcuts. This may come in the form of temptation to do something illegal, immoral, or unethical. These temptations may come in a form of illegal kickbacks, quality misinformation, price gouging, and many other things.

As a reminder, you will have lenders, investors, customers, and eventually employees who will expect you to always do the right thing, always be loyal to them and represent them in the most trustworthy way. This may be the reason why they decided to join you in the first place, as they felt that you were a person worthy of trust. However, if you failed at being loyal to them, they would either leave, create legal issues, or become angry—and this could within itself become your demise. Always remain loyal, no matter what. It's a long road and the journey to success is littered with failed individuals who forgot about loyalty—or had none from the beginning.

Keep in mind that there is nothing easy about the road to success; it's a long hard slough, and it will not be easy for anyone to cross the finish line. If you don't have an idea about loyalty, especially in a business setting, there are classes that you can take on this subject. This writer strongly suggests that any innovator wanting to succeed educate themselves on this very important subject matter, especially in today's highly competitive and complex world that is full of regulations made to safeguard the public. Safeguarding the public means that we must always strive to love thy neighbors!

LOVE

Many individuals live by the motto of the "Golden Rule." For those who have never heard about the Golden Rule, it represents having love and respect for your fellow person. The Golden Rule is practiced by the motto of treating others as you would want to be treated.

Love is a word that can come in various forms—for example, love toward your friends, love toward your children, love toward your parents, love toward your siblings, love toward your spouse, or even love of food, etc. It may be so strong that it would make us do things like, give up our own lives for it. It can also mean that we would be willing to give everything we possess to keep it and not lose it. There are still other individuals who are willing to purchase love with money or material possessions in order to acquire it. The different forms of love can come with different forms of sacrifice. Some of these are individuals willing to donate live organs to their loved ones, regardless of the risk. Love is a very powerful motivator, and can many times be the culprit or motivator of any individual's success or demise.

The innovator must love what they do, for without love you will never be happy and reach your goal of success. Love is a very powerful passion and will make the difference between success and failure. So, before you begin your journey to success, make sure that you are in love with your innovation. This will help facilitate things when you are presenting to others. Just as we love introducing our families to our friends, in the same way, your innovation will be easy to share with others. Love is also a form of compassion towards others, so as you grow your team and company, you will want to "spread the love" among your employees—meaning that you ensure good wages, good benefits, a safe work environment, etc.

From the time that we share our love with others, others will be made aware of it, and your reputation will soar from the fact that you are willing to share your success with others. This is also a form of showing your love for your fellow person. You will benefit from sharing with others in the long term, and your journey to success will become that much easier to obtain. However, this takes courage to think about what the future holds. You must have hope that everything will be fine, even if you share your success with others.

COURAGE

Courage is one of the most sought-after traits in a human. Courage has the ability to reflect as confidence, and confidence is very important at all times. In business, this is a trait that you must possess! Never think that you can become successful if you do not possess this trait. The reason for this is that when in a fight or battle, those surrounded by courageous individuals will be confident that they are protected and will be backed up till the end. This, in turn, makes the unit fight even harder and with more confidence in victory. If you suspect that this is a trait that you do not possess or that you altogether lack, then you must acquire this trait before you get started on your journey to success. There are mental exercises that you can practice, and you must practice overcoming fear—that is what courage means. So if you lack courage, get started at once with your exercises.

Simple suggestions of how to do this are:

1. Writing down situations that cause fears.

2. Never comparing yourself with others.
3. Always embracing the positive things in life and avoid the negative things at all cost.
4. Believing in yourself and having confidence that you can be courageous.
5. Being willing to take risks and accept failure.

Having or gaining courage will also allow you to become a leader. This will be very important as you begin to progress along your journey to success. As you begin to attempt to convince others about the value that your innovation brings to the marketplace, and what a great opportunity it represents for them, courage will become a very important part inside your tool bag—especially when you experience pushback. Courage will help you gain confidence as you build a team around you that you can train on exactly how to execute your idea or innovation.

Even beyond convincing a team, courage will help you have confidence when you are pitching your idea to potential customers. Some of these settings can become intimidating for those that don't have courage. Courage is like a muscle; it must be exercised and worked on. There are no shortcuts. Therefore, to create courage and confidence, you must always prepare and practice your presentation, making sure that you are 100 percent familiar with the information that you will be presenting. This will ensure that your message will gain traction on your journey to success.

Passion

Passion is a strong desire that can get you to do amazing things! It is something that drives an individual to seek whatever it is that they are trying to secure. If the individual were to fall down in pursuit of his or her goal, it is passion that would help get the individual get up and get back in pursuit of the goal. See, without passion there could be no courage, no love, and no success. Passion causes us to possess and exercise the other traits that are needed in order to succeed. Without passion, a human can become unhappy, bored and dissatisfied with life. They call passion the "zest of life," so one must try to enjoy life with zest at all times and in all places, whenever possible.

If you are feeling like you have lost the zest for life, maybe you need to think of activities that can help you get that passion back. You can try health and fitness, learning, improving your personal growth, travel, catching up with past relationships or starting new relationships, using your creativity, etc. If your innovation has matured, maybe you can start a new innovation, education, etc.

You have to do whatever it takes to never lose passion, always making sure that you have passion for what you do. Again, if you find yourself bored and without zest, do whatever you have to do to get it back. Sometimes it simply takes getting some time off from your frantic daily schedule and having change of scenery for a week or two. After you are rested and refreshed, you may find out that it was the only thing you needed. If that still does not do it, then it may be something more fundamental, and you must take the steps to address it. Passion and patience are inherently linked to each other. Passion is a trait that carries or motivates one to move forward, and patience ensures that if the goal is taking a bit too long, you stay on track, regardless of the time or the effort that your goal will require to be achieved.

PATIENCE

Innovation can come in different forms. For example, it may be a product, a new process of making something, or a new business model. Because innovation comes in different forms, some innovation takes longer and more patience is required. Your idea may require more capital, or another idea or innovation may require a much more technical approach. Whatever the case, patience is very necessary to acquire success.

There is a story about the time that Thomas Edison was working on inventing the light bulb. At the time, he still had not succeeded. When speaking about his progress, he said, "I have not failed. I've just found 10,000 ways that won't work." This shows the patience and, at times, the maddening effect and effort that it can ultimately take to create a successful innovation. Sometimes it might be simply convincing others about your idea; however, this within itself may prove to be much more difficult than it might appear.

There is a saying that "Rome was not built in a day." Rome is a beautiful city, full of great architecture and culture. The Romans were famous for creating and planning these projects, sometimes many years in advance. Sometimes in order to gain victory, they would build great projects just to eventually overcome their opponents. These projects could take much planning, engineering, labor, money, and material; however, eventually they would succeed and eventually gain victory. Again, patience is what it takes. If you sometimes find yourself tired in pursuit of your innovation, it's fine to take a break for a few days or weeks and get back to it. After you are refreshed, however, never forget your goal.

One of this writer's favorite stories of patience is a story about a young man's love for his girlfriend. After he asked her family for her hand in marriage, the father told him that he would give his daughters hand in marriage under one condition. The condition was that he would have to work for his future father-in-law for a total of seven years, and only then could he marry the daughter. The young man eagerly agreed and worked for a total of seven years for his future father-in-law. The wedding was planned and performed. But there was a problem—when the young man saw his newlywed wife the next morning, he suddenly realized that it was her sister that he had spent his honeymoon with! He immediately addressed his father-in law and requested an explanation about how this trickery and confusion between sisters could have possibly have happened. The father-in-law said, "Oh, on the contrary, there is no confusion, for it is customary in our culture to always have the oldest daughter marry first."

The father-in law then proceeded to say that he had an easy solution. All this desperate and broken-hearted young man had to do was agree to work for an additional seven years to marry the girl of his dreams, who he deeply loved. The young man again agreed, and worked for his father-in law for seven years. The wedding day finally came, and after 14 years of waiting, he was finally married to the love of his life. What a story of love and passion, but more than anything else, patience! Do you have the patience to work hard for 14 years just to get what you want out of life? During these modern times, in your case you might already be with your loved one, but are you willing to work for fourteen years on your journey to success?

No doubt that the journey to success will require, planning, strategy, hope, courage, passion, love, patience, and more. You will need to plan to ensure the odds of success heavily favor you. So don't forget that planning is half the journey!

Preparing for the Journey to Success

Again, as with any travel, we must be prepared to bring all the things that will help us make our journey successful. Not only the physical tools that we may need, like boots, clothes, water, food, a compass, etc., but we also need to carry within us psychological tools that we need, like courage, passion, love, hope, courage, patience, etc.

Before we get started, we need to do a checklist or evaluation of all the items that we will need. Without this, our journey may become disastrous. Remember, the journey that lies ahead is full of booby traps, potholes, harsh weather, nasty people, predator-infested areas, etc. Dangers lurk around every corner.

Securing food, shelter, and personal security will be a daily challenge during your journey, and without these items you risk becoming just another victim. You must have a plan of entry and a plan for an exit, just as well. If you are to travel with others, make sure that these individuals are well-equipped all around as well, and that they possess the skills to survive all the challenges that will be coming your way.

As Abraham Lincoln said when talking about preparation, "I will prepare and someday my chances will come." Another Lincoln quote about preparation is, "Give me six hours to chop down a tree and I spend the first four sharpening the axe." This helps us understand just how important planning for success is. If the most successful president in American history prepared this way, it is easy to understand how he was able to succeed in such a big way.

LET'S GET GOING

As you begin your travel planning, you will need to know your starting point and your exit point. Without this, you risk the danger of being in disarray or disoriented. So that this does not happen, you must know the plan ahead of time. That way, if you have a group of friends or family members, this will ensure that all these individuals will be working in harmony towards a common goal. Leadership is something that you will have to have if you are to navigate your team through predator-infested regions along your trip. Remember, the terrain is full of wild predators that can attack at any time—and when you least expect it.

But why does this writer talk so much about predators? For the simple reason that they are there waiting to ruin your plans of success. They come in the form of competitors, family, friends or employees, or even co-workers. The road to success is littered with innovators' carcasses, eaten and left to rot by cannibals. Don't be a victim! You must always be aware of your surroundings. You must possess defensive weapons and use speed to neutralize all these dangers.

Now, let's get started!

So, You're Ready to Become a Successful Innovator

The beginnings of how to become a successful innovator have something to do with either chance or necessity. Velcro is a perfect example of chance. It has since become one of the most successful fasteners known to man and is now used in industries around the world. In this case, it so happens that a simple walk through the fields started this innovation. What happened next is that the Velcro innovator got his socks full of small thorns. Just like many other innovators would have done, his curiosity led him to investigate more closely as to how it was possible that such a small thorn could possibly pack such a huge grip. So he looked at it through a microscope, and in amazement saw that the thorn had multiple little curved hooks that caught the loops formed within the woven textile construction of his socks. This gave the innovator the idea it might be a way of creating a great fastener. The innovator's hunch was right, and the rest is history!

However, necessity works differently—it is the most common method of innovating. Companies are constantly studying the ways that they can innovate their current product lines, and therefore, many of their employees are allowed big budgets in order to innovate. In the case of an entrepreneur, the innovation may come from two things. The first is the desire to improve his or her economic situation, and the knowledge that he or she possesses from a certain industry. If you are an entrepreneur that is just warming to the idea of innovating, you are likely on a shoestring budget—or you have no budget at all. If this is the case, it's very necessary that you resort back to the memories of when you were younger and the times that you were willing to do anything to earn and save money to buy that bike that you wanted or your first car or whatever the item that you felt that you were in need of at the time. Some of the jobs that you were willing to do were not well paid or not exactly what you would prefer to do, but you did them anyway because you really wanted that item so badly that there was no other way to get it. You might even be willing to hold a second job to accomplish the purchase of that specific item. Yes, innovation takes much sacrifice. If washing dishes in a restaurant is what it will take, or serving tables, this is what you must do until you have a budget or the seed money needed to begin your innovation.

If, by chance, you are a good promoter or salesperson, then in your case you may have the ability to get a loan or talk some individuals into becoming your investors. However, most people have a hard time talking about money, especially with strangers. Yet for others, this may be the quickest way to accomplish your goal. If you have a problem talking to others about money, you must practice and get comfortable at being able to do so. This is a very important step to gain traction on your road to success, especially when you begin to promote your innovation to others.

As you get closer to your planned launch day, you must know which method or path you will take. Will it be a loan, investor money, or extra proceeds from moonlighting?

The path or method that you have chosen has much to do with the next items or tools that you must acquire. If you will be pursuing a loan through a bank, you will need a few things. First you will need a personal financial statement. You will also need some form of collateral or some form of equity to secure the loan in case you would not be able to pay the loan back. You may also need a written business plan.

If you are pursuing an investor, you must equip yourself with a solid written business plan, a projection or forecast of potential future sales, and what the monies will be used for. This writer highly recommends a professional, well-detailed PowerPoint that will enhance or complement your presentation or pitch. This PowerPoint needs to have an introduction, and cover topics like what the idea is, what the idea resolves, the projection for sales will be and how much time it will take to accomplish, what the proceeds will be used for, and what the method or strategy will be going forward so as to hit the projected numbers.

If you have a savings plan that you can turn to, then it is still highly recommended to create a written business plan so that you can measure the results versus your forecast. The written business plan will also ensure that you always have a reminder that you can review at any time allowing the possibility of sharing the vision and plan with others as you begin to grow your team all around you.

SELLING THE IDEA

Don't worry when you read the title of this section—it does not mean that you will be selling your idea, of course, if you don't wish to go that route. Most innovators like to see their idea through, and most feel that no one will do as good as a job as they can. As the saying goes, "This is their baby." If the idea works and becomes an economic success, it is likely that competitors will offer to buy it; however, this will be a different topic that we will cover later on in the book.

The selling of the idea means explaining it to others or giving the pitch to see if a loan or an investment can be secured. The innovator must make a huge effort to practice the pitch so that he or she is 100 percent comfortable with all the material that will be covered. Part of a successful pitch is presenting an attractive and professional PowerPoint that is to the point and keeps the viewer interested. Keep in mind that every bank or investor has its own criteria, and make sure that you inquire what these are. Some may have a criteria with a smaller deal, others may prefer a criteria that covers a deal with larger amounts, and yet others may want nothing to do with startups all together. Keep all this in mind so that you don't waste your time or the other people's time as well. Never present or pitch knowing that the criteria is not lined up with your business plan and projected forecast.

There may be times where the conversation will cover the possibilities of whether you're willing to make the product in some other country and if this is something you would be willing to do, or if you would be willing to be flexible or change your idea or business plan up a bit. These may be make-or-break decisions, and this writer recommends that the innovator not rush into a quick yes or no decision. The best response would be that any issues brought to light will be taken into consideration by you and will be addressed at a later time but as soon possible.

TOOLING UP

Right from the beginning of your journey, you will need something that conveys your idea. This means that you must work on some type of prototype or sampling. If your innovation is a product, the way to start is with drawings that can convey the idea. As you will need to seek help with the construction and manufacturing and equipment and material that will be required to make it, you will need a more technical approach. If you do not have the software expertise, you can hire a local designer who can start with some digital drawings. These will also have to be in a 3D design format to include full rotation for side views and top bottom views of the product. If you are innovating a business concept, you will also need drawings that convey the idea. However, creating vivid drawings or renderings might be enough, and you may not need a digital-type presentation. A graphic artist may be able to help you with this.

After you have secured the drawings of your innovation, you will then be prepared to proceed to talking with experts in the given industry. They will be able to advise you on the next steps needed to make your samples. You may also need to source materials, as well. The sampling process is altogether a different a different process and will require that you talk to prototype experts. Now, this does not mean that your prototype will be identical to your final product, but it will be a close enough representation that you will be able to hold it in your hand, giving you a good feel for your product. After this phase is over with, you will have a prototype that you will be able to show your network of experts, like patent attorneys, mold-makers, sales personnel, customers, etc.

This may also allow you to start promoting your product at tradeshows to measure interest and market intelligence before taking a full-on risk and going all the way. We will cover how to go about this later on in the book. Allowing others to see your product will allow a touch-and-feel approach, and this will help you decide if you feel that there is enough interest for your innovation or not. This writer is a firm believer in allowing the market to touch and feel a sample of my innovation, preferably at tradeshows, therefore gauging the interest within the industry.

THE TRADE SHOW

Getting ready for a tradeshow requires many decisions that must be made in a timely manner. These tradeshows come in different sizes, as some are regional, others national and yet others international. The cost is directly associated with the attendance that the show will bring. This writer recommends that your introductory trade show begin with a regional show. This writer also recommends that you start with a regional show that is close to where you live so that you do not have to spend a lot of money on travel. You will also need to prepay for the space that you need ahead of time. You will have to decide and work on a display to show your products' applications for all to be able to view. There is a whole host of other things that you must plan and work on before displaying at the trade show. Below is a list of the items that you must take with you.

1. Brochures with a picture and the trade name of your product, a brief description of your product and what it does, the sizes it comes in, the colors it comes in, the model numbers, either a patent pending or patent number, etc.
2. A business card with your company name, your personal name, title, address and phone number.
3. Clipboards for filling out the survey.
4. Number 2 pencils with erasers
5. A quick and easy, fun-to-fill-out survey that will be have not more than five multiple choice questions.

5a. The first question recommended is: Is this a product you would be willing to use?

5b. The second question recommended is: How much would you be willing to pay for this product?

5c. The third question recommended is: What are you using right now?

5d. The fourth question recommended is: Would you recommend this to your customers?

5e. The fifth recommended question is: Where do you usually purchase this type of product?

As a reminder, to ensure success you must always dress professionally for the tradeshow and be well groomed, as you will be the face of your company and of your offering.

After the Trade Show

After the tradeshow you will have a good idea of whether you will continue to pursue your innovation or not. If not, you need to move on immediately and not linger on it. You can move into another idea or take a break before you make your next move. However, if the level of interest was high and you have decided to pursue your innovation, you will then have to move into the product-manufacturing phase.

This writer recommends that if you feel that you have a winner, it is very important to use stealth speed to bring your product into the marketplace. Keep in mind that any potential competitor more than likely will be aware of your innovation. Some competitors will see your product as a danger to their market, while others may just be greedy and feel that they can beat you to the marketplace. Welcome to the jungle, my friend! Remember that we had mentioned that sometimes you will have to move with speed? Well, this is one of those phases that requires speed. Therefore, you must get ready to make your product, package and price it, and put it out to market.

There are additional things to consider within this phase of introduction. It may be smart to hire a local sales representative to help you show and sell your product. There are sales organizations that work off of commissions that may be willing to pioneer your product line; however, be prepared to work on finding the right fit, as many organizations do not like doing pioneer work and are ill-prepared to do so.

As you go into the marketplace and show your products, you will have to know the type of channel that your product will sell in. Some may be retail, and yet another channel maybe a distribution channel. Whatever it may be, you may find out that your product has a high degree of acceptance even with the retailers or the distributors. However, before you strike a deal, you might have to consider that there will be issues thrown your way before they make a commitment to buy. These may come in all types of forms, like extended purchasing terms, guaranteed buy-back in case that the product does not sell, promotional allowances, and the much-dreaded deep discounts. If you do decide to come to terms with this, it is more than likely that you will eventually have a deal, depending on their technical committees or their sales force opinions. However, given that you have come this far down the road, it is more than likely that you will strike a deal. Congratulations—you are well on your way to success!

The customer will ask you for sales and promotional support artwork, so you must make sure that you have a good photo taken of your product, and promote it within the customer's literature or promotional materials, and also their website. Being first to market is a huge advantage in the marketplace and should ensure that your customer base will become very loyal to your product. The overall measure of the success of your product will ultimately be repeat sales; however, we will cover this later on in the book.

Promoting the Innovation

So, the race is officially on!

Know that the sooner that you can ramp up production the better. You must now move quickly to form a national sales team that will help promote and sell your product and pitch your innovation. Remember that the competition is well aware of your new product and is now watching you and monitoring your progress. You will more than likely need to travel to meet and qualify the different individuals who will comprise your sales team. Just like hiring an employee, you need to request references and especially what lines they are currently representing. The most important thing to consider is whether any of their current lines create a conflict with your product. If this is the case, you must resist doing the deal with this individual. The ideal sales representative will be introducing you to their best customers in the region, and they will be following up on the progress to strike a deal.

The sales organization will do promotional marketing at the local trade shows after you have left and also follow up on leads that have demonstrated interest. Some of this will require pull-through marketing. Once your sales organization is formed, you will be prepared to attend and display your innovation at the national tradeshows. You will have to plan and budget this type of tradeshow, as the costs can be exorbitant. After you have chosen the space and the size of your display booth, you must decide what kind of display you will have. There are some design companies that can help you with the design and construction—and even the logistics and set-up—of the display. Again, you will have to budget for this, as the investment will be substantial. You will also require a travel budget and plan for the personnel who will be required to tend to the tradeshow attendees. The personnel must be friendly and approachable; they must also be well-trained and informed about your innovation and have the ability to explain the innovation in a detailed and concise way. They must also be able to gather personal information from the attendees who express interest and process the leads. There is a form of scanner that can also facilitate this process, and you can rent this type of system from the expo's exhibiting offices.

After the trade show you will have to process each individual lead and begin the process of pull-through marketing with your salesforce. Each lead should contain detailed information about the contact, and also whether samples were requested or offered. This is very important to follow up on, as attendees will not forget if they made a request and no one followed up with them. The easiest way to do this is to forward the leads to the sales representatives who represents you in their given region for a quick follow-up. Also make sure that you request an update after the contact has been approached so you can continue to gauge the interest or the level of progress made.

OTHER INDUSTRY INFLUENCERS

Each industry has its own type of influencers. These are not customers, per se, but they are an integral part of the process of reaching out to the mass markets or influencing others on the purchase of products. They can come in all forms like buyers, consultants, media personal, sales representatives, industry lobbyists, etc. It is very important to treat these individuals with respect and just like a customer, for they will sometimes be able to help you grow your business in a very substantial way. At trade shows, the media sales personnel are the most active and are networking with potential customers. These are the folks who work for the industry magazines. They have thousands of established readers throughout the country, and usually come out with new monthly editions that inform the industry about the different things that are happening.

This will be your contact list so that you can then start mass marketing and advertising your innovation. Remember, the sooner that you do this the better.

Being the first to market carries a lot of benefits in the long run. So reach out to these influencers and stay in touch with them; they will be more than happy to help you formulate a media campaign for your innovation, as they love to inform their readers about new concepts or products in the industry. The formulation of a media campaign will include the number of readers that this magazine will reach, so you will be able to assess if it is something that you are interested in or not. Some magazines have limited in coverage to certain regions and may have a smaller readership count, while other magazines have national coverage and have a much larger coverage and readership base.

The media person will also give you the breakdown of what type of readership their magazine has. This is an important consideration for you, as it means that you can focus within a certain group within the industry, if that is what you're looking for. The magazine company will also have a way of providing information in the form of a lead. Again, this will give your sales organization a constant pipeline of fresh leads to approach, helping them with their sales efforts in their regions.

By now, you should have a good idea about what advertising message you will need to produce and how to raise the maximum amount of interest possible. You will need to hire a graphic artist who can help you design an attractive advertising ad. This will have to have a high-resolution photograph of your product and of the graphics and logos that you will use. It will also have to have your company phone number and your website address. Magazine advertising can be quite pricey, so you will have to also possibly start with a smaller-sized advertising, and as the business grows then purchase and secure larger sized advertising.

Your industry may have more than one magazine; some may concentrate on certain submarket or another, while some may concentrate on certain type of professionals only. You will have to decide which is the best-suited magazine or advertising vehicle for your innovation.

COMPETITION

The good, the bad, and the ugly. Yes, competition comes in this manner! As you begin to get more exposure with your innovation, you may begin to have incidents that will be direct and at times difficult to deal with. With tradeshows, it will not be difficult for a competitor to walk over to your booth and express some form of aggression towards you. This writer has experienced this and advises you to stay very vigilant, especially during tradeshows. When you are addressed by competitors, the smartest approach is to keep your thoughts to yourself and don't give the competition any clue about your market progress or your innovation's success. If some form of aggression is displayed to you, always respond with a kindness and try to disengage as soon as possible.

At times, there will be other competitors who will express outright anger, as they are frustrated with your success in the marketplace. If faced with this situation, keep in mind that you must avoid it altogether.

Some competitors will tell you about the frustrations that they are currently experiencing with other competitors and will give you details in the ways they are being harassed or even being pressured into a deal. Now, this is something that you do not need at a tradeshow. A tradeshow setting should be a positive experience; however, we cannot control our competition, so you must do everything in your power to only network with the individuals who are positive industry people.

On the other hand, there will be some competitors who may confide that you have a better innovation than they do, and that you have beat them to the punch. You also want to make sure that you do not revel in this and limit your conversation with these types of individuals, as well. You see, in life there is a saying: "You reap what you sow." Naturally, we do not want to sow despair for anyone as this may lead to our own despair. Take this in stride and keep going!

The journey to success is full of booby traps that are set up by our competitors. Be very vigilant at all times and remember that intelligence will be required at all times. You never want to become a victim of a booby trap, as once you are down it is very hard to recover. Also, you must always be careful about who you're talking to, as you never know what relationship one individual may have with another.

DISTRACTIONS

During your journey to success there will be discussions and temptations that have the potential to distract any innovator. As you gain momentum in the marketplace, your confidence will soar, and you may become content. Always remember that you are running a marathon; it's a long, hard slough, not a short, easy sprint. There have been many innovators who, once they feel economic security, resort to behaviors of pleasure and begin to prioritize passing many hours away from the office, spending them on personal activities that have nothing to do with the business. It is understandable that, from time to time, there will be a moment to take a customer or a prospective customer to play golf or some other activity that will allow both parties to get to know each other. But don't get lured in by others to waste your precious valuable time while you are still on your journey to success. You will have all the time you desire after you're done with your journey and you have succeeded. Wasting valuable time and not building your business will allow the competition to get closer to catching up and bypassing you in the marketplace.

There are a few sayings about wasting time; the first one that comes to this writer's mind is, "Someone wasting your time is far worse than someone wasting your money." The other one is, "Wasting time is robbing Oneself." One saying concludes that time is worth much more that money. The other saying concludes that wasting time ends up being like robbing yourself. How tragic! You see, a successful innovation is worth millions, if not billions, of dollars! Anything or anyone that gets in your way and wastes your time should be avoided at all cost. Albert Einstein was a big believer in the idea that every minute of extra time spent on making decisions about what to wear was a waste of time, so he made it a practice to always wear a different variation of the same gray-colored suit every morning. This was one of the smartest people in the history of the world, so if Albert Einstein thought about this and practiced it, it really meant that wasted time—even a single extra minute—should be avoided, as the costs will be exorbitant.

OVERCONFIDENCE

As you get to the first stages of success, you will possibly experience what many innovators experience. These can include feelings of invisibility, overconfidence, loftiness, untouchable-ness, or a sense of "I can make no mistakes!" See, as the innovator reaches a certain stage of success, many individuals will tell him or her how great and smart they are. This can become intoxicating and can lead to a big head.

There was once a Greek king called Midas. He made a wish to one of the Greek gods and the wish was granted. His wish was that everything that he touched would turn to gold. Delighted, he began to convert twigs, stones, apples and other food items. Rejoicing, the next morning he grabbed a rose to smell the fragrance, but the rose become gold. Midas said, "I will have to smell the fragrance of the rose without touching it." As he prepared to enjoy breakfast, his bread turned into gold as he prepared to eat it, and his wine converted to gold as he began to drink it. Midas realized that his wish had become a curse. He also happened to touch his daughter, converting her into gold. He immediately asked the god to reverse the wish, which was also granted. He was instructed to wash in Pactolus river, which he did, leaving all the gold in the sand. Everything that he had converted to gold was converted back. The lesson taught King Midas a lesson about the dangers of overconfidence, loftiness, and greed. He once possessed the ability to convert everything that he touched into gold, yet he asked for the wish to be reversed as the cost proved too high, without a doubt. The story ends in that after the bad experience, King Midas became a much more compassionate king, and his people prospered under his rule for many years.

We would be smart in learning from these stories, even though they are myths, the great danger that can come from overconfidence and loftiness. As humans, we must always keep these types of feelings in check, for entire countries and cultures have been lost and ruined by not keeping a check on the human trait of grandiosity.

GRANDIOSITY AND STUBBORNESS

This writer once had a meeting with an innovator who was seeking help with beginning his new and exciting line of barbecue grills. He had secured a meeting with one of this writer's sons through contact with one of our computer vendors. As a favor, we accommodated him and his girlfriend. After being introduced and exchanging niceties, this writer asked the innovator to tell us about himself, to which the innovator responded, "I have been in the barbeque grill business for many years, and I know the business very well!" He was very emphatic about his experience.

The writer then asked him if he was presently selling grills, to which he replied that he was presently selling real estate; however, he had been a very successful businessman who had sold hundreds of grills in the past. He was so sure that his innovation would be a success because his would be lighter, mobile, have infrared technology, and have a superior design. The writer asked him about his price point, and he mentioned that it would be a high-end product and that it would cost substantially more than competitors' brands currently being offered in the marketplace because of this.

The writer asked the innovator about any drawings that he may have brought that would convey his idea. The innovator responded that no, he had no drawings, or even sketches, at the moment. He also mentioned that he was looking for a company that would help design his invention, and that he would sit down with the designer assigned and dictate or convey how the features were to be integrated into his design. This was the way he was proposing to work and invent.

Fast forward, the writer asked a series of questions in an effort to help the innovator see the big picture. The questions went as so: Why do you want to do this? Are you willing to do this regardless of the risk involved? If you are presently employed with a decent and secure salary selling real estate, why would you want to do this? Do you realize that the barbecue grill business is a very crowded field?

The innovator responded assertively after every question, saying, "I have so much experience in the barbecue grill business that I am sure that my innovation will be a huge success!" Well, we all know that success is not guaranteed. When the writer and his son saw this innovator shut his mind off and become stubborn, we started to dig deeper. Part of this book is about the need for planning and budgeting. The innovator had come to the meeting with no plan other than saying that his innovation was better! The innovator also had mentioned that he had gone broke previously. He obviously had already experienced the taste of defeat; however, he continued telling the writer and his son that he was not afraid of taking risk, regardless of whatever the cost would be.

A wise man once told his followers, "Suppose one of you wants to build a tower. Won't you sit down and estimate the cost to see if you have enough money to complete it? For if you lay the foundation and are not able to finish it, everyone who sees it will ridicule you, saying "This person began to build and wasn't able to finish."

The sad thing about the above-mentioned innovator is that he did not have a budget, either! No sketches and no budgets, yet he kept saying that he did not fear risk! At that point, the writer pushed back, feeling that he was witnessing grandiosity and stubbornness and sensing that this person was just about to trip over a precipice! "So," the writer exclaimed, "don't you realize that you are going into the jungle and it's infested with cannibals? You are about to be eaten alive, and your carcass will be left for all the wild animals to eat!" The writer then continued, "Don't you see that your competitors see this as not necessarily a competition about innovation or even money, but a blood sport? Like the gladiators of the past, they fought just for sport!" To which the innovator replied that the writer was depressing him.

The writer responded that being positive is a good thing; however, the emphasis on only being positive and not on what can go wrong could be a recipe for disaster. The innovator's girlfriend shrugged her shoulders and said that the innovator did not like working for anyone else. The innovator then asked the writer if he would enjoy working for anyone else, to which the writer responded, "Not at all!" The innovator thanked the writer and his son for their time and mentioned that he would be in back in contact.

The takeaway from this experience is that without a plan and a budget, any innovator is bound to fail—and that not being willing to do so will ensure being eaten alive by competitors. Again, grandiosity and stubbornness will get you killed every single time!

UNPLANNED INNOVATION
CAN HAVE CONSEQUENCES

Innovation may promote a whole host of human emotional and physical issues, as well. These may come in the form of pressure, anxiety, restlessness, insomnia, depression, and may be associated with other physical health issues like high blood pressure, shortness of breath, heart failure, stomach issues, headaches, etc.

This writer has known and experienced some of the above issues as part of his challenges during his time of innovation. Just the knowing that you have a lot riding on the success of your innovation, and the question of whether you will either succeed or fail, has everything to do with experiencing these types of health issues.

The writer not only writes from his own experiences as an innovator, but also after witnessing other innovators' hardships. In the case of this writer, he actually saw an innovator go firsthand through health consequences when trying to further his progress on his innovation. Between the writer's son and the innovator, there had been some work done. The problem started when the innovator had an idea for improvement of his product—mostly in his head, not on paper. In addition to this, not only was his previous design done by others, but he had previously sent the molds of changes to be made on his existing product line overseas. The molds would not work properly and had been failing. He had also asked this writer's son to help him with some of his molded parts, which he had also been manufacturing overseas. With all the pressure of not being able to come up with consistent product quality, and not being able to resolve things quickly, he appeared to be suffering from the physical and emotional consequences of innovating.

You see, the innovator was under much pressure because his current product was not consistent in quality, and along with that, there was a competitor who had made a similar product with consistent quality at a lower price. On top of that, the competitor had taken a substantial part of the innovator's business. As the pressures mounted, he started to blame everyone around him, including this writer's son, for all his innovation problems. After going through this for several months, one day the writer's son told the innovator that he was not going to help him with his project anymore, including improving the design. The next day, this writer saw the innovator come to his offices looking for the writer's son to ask him to reconsider. The son continued to hold fast to his decision.

That day, the innovator looked like he was under so much physical and emotional strain that the writer, out of pity, asked his son to continue to help the innovator. But his son still respectfully refused. Believe it or not, that same night the innovator had a massive heart attack and ended up in the hospital! The writer's son, being a young man, did not realize that the innovator had everything on the line and the difference of success or failure could have on him and his family. Of course failure brought huge, negative consequences!

Now, the writer's son was also a good friend of the family. They understood the difficulties of working along the innovator and had expressed them to the writer's son many times before, so there was no blame expressed at the writer's son. However, the writer's son felt so bad about the desperate situation that the innovator was in, fighting for his life, that he began to help the innovator after he got out of the hospital and began to fully recover.

That story has always been in this writer's thoughts, and it is the first thing that comes to his mind when innovators reach out to him and begin to talk to him about the innovation process. The common thread among some innovators is that they don't stop to plan or strategize. They rest on their laurels because of the so-called vast experience they possess, and they begin to take shortcuts, expecting that others will do much of their work. However, they possess no manufacturing, processing or engineering experience or knowledge most of the time, and this is where they confuse experience within the industry that they have been involved in with experience pertaining to the part of innovation that requires manufacturing.

The need for you to become totally educated about your innovation is crucial, and becoming familiar with materials, process, and design is crucial for the success of your product. All innovators must invest time in becoming familiar with this part of the journey, especially before seeking help from other professionals who will need much more clarity. As the saying goes, save yourself a lot of heartache!

THE HIGH VALUE
OF EDUCATION BEFORE INNOVATION

If you are an innovator with education in your background, it's more than likely that you will be innovating something within your field of expertise. It is the innovator that possesses no education who usually needs more help during the design, prototype, and manufacturing process. The innovator who plans to succeed needs to educate him or herself before starting the innovation process. This may include taking college courses, trade school training, or special reading on subjects that pertain to the innovation. Many times, going to tradeshows can also serve as education, as the innovator can ask many technical questions, and many times the manufacturers will have a team of engineers ready to answer them. The innovator has to be constantly in search of cutting-edge information so he or she can integrate the knowledge they've acquired into the innovation.

Not only is the value of an education with a degree important for advancing the innovation through the design, prototype, and manufacturing phases, education also helps validate the innovation to other professionals, especially bankers, lenders, and potential investors. The innovators' resume and educational background must always be a part of any presentation given for all the aforementioned reasons. This will keep the listener much more engaged and serious in respect to the odds that the innovation has value. See, innovation is the mother's milk of business; when successful, it leads to economic progress and prosperity. So, as an innovator, always keep in mind that regardless of how well companies do with their respective existing products, they must be constantly innovating in order to continue to offer their customers new and exciting products.

The writer realizes that the educational process can take time, money, and a lot of energy. However, this must be part of the innovation process and will dramatically increase the chances of success. Even if the innovator comes from humble beginnings or the poorest situations, areas or countries, you must make the sacrifice, as possessing an education will change the odds and the trajectory of success in your favor.

ASSEMBLING THE TEAM

Keep in mind that first-time entrepreneurs only have an 18 percent chance of success. This means that the odds of failure are 82 percent! If you are among the few innovators that have succeeded and are reading this book, I salute you! However, don't relax, for there is still much work to do!

Again, if you are one of the fortunate innovators who have succeeded, you will have to put together a team of helpers who will help you educate others and promote your new innovation. Therefore, you will have to advertise each position that you will be offering. You will also need to interview all the individuals who will be applying for the positions. A good start would be to post the job on Indeed.com or ZipRecruiter.com. You can become a member for a nominal fee. Some of these services will even do a match-up and give you the odds of a perfect match, which may be helpful in making your final decisions.

Your job posting must always contain a brief description of your business. It must always require a minimum level of education, willingness to travel, professional appearance, experience in sales, and good writing, computer and communication skills. The job posting may or may not contain salary or benefits information, as this may be considered on an individual and or private basis if you prefer. The individual chosen must be a very quick learner, be friendly and be easy to approach. This will ensure that your message will be well-received by others and that your innovation will be accepted throughout the industry.

Before you attempt to assemble a team, you will need to provide a professional-looking office space that will be equipped with all the necessary phone systems, computer systems, desks, chairs, conference room, restroom facilities and an employee lounge. This will be important, as the applicants will also be observing and thinking about whether or not they will want to work for you from the moment they walk through the door. Keep in mind that the most valuable employees are the ones who expect all these things from an employer, as they also value their time and effort.

Once you have assembled the team, you will have to have your strategy in your mind well founded, and you must have this strategy written down for others to be able to discuss, understand and follow. The preparation of this is so important that it will serve to facilitate an understanding of your strategy and will make getting to the meeting of the minds much easier. The strategy must also contain goals or targets that will have to be met so that the company continues to succeed into the future. Your plan will have to also contain targeted areas that your team is to focus their efforts on to bring quicker success, and where you already have the highest chance of succeeding.

This writer also had to go through assembling a team. However, before doing so, he looked for an applicant that could be entrusted with many chores, including running the business itself. This happened to be his brother-in-law. It just so happened that the business was growing at a fast pace, and his brother-in-law was looking for a job at the time. So, after agreeing on an employment contract, they started to discuss what was needed to continue to keep up with the business's growth. Without a doubt, it was to begin assembling our own production. The writer knew that this would not be any easy task; however, they stayed on course with the expansion project. It just so happens, in retrospect, that it was one of the best decisions ever made. As profits soared, costs of production were reduced, shipping of product quickened, availability of inventory improved, and quality improved.

Yes, assembling your team can be overwhelming just to think about, however, the benefits are just too many just to be ignored.

Assembling Your Production

Eventually you will have to decide, if your innovation is a product, where it will be manufactured. Keep in mind that some industries are more sensitive to importing products than others. This needs to be part of the information-gathering that you must do before making your final decision. You may have to depend on subcontractors to supply you with inventory in the beginning; however, when the demand for your product increases dramatically, you may have to secure your own equipment. If you are thinking long-term, this may be your best choice. As competitors begin to enter your field, this may be a good decision that will help you control costs, maintain inventories, and continue a high standard of quality.

The manufacturing process can be an expensive, time-consuming, and difficult process to begin. However, it can also be very rewarding, and proper planning will ensure that you will be successful in the manufacturing business if this is what you decide to do.

There are many regulations that control manufacturing and depending on what area of the country that you plan to do business in, you may or may not be able to secure the business permits. If not, you will have to find an area that welcomes your type of manufacturing.

You will have to also assemble a production team to begin your manufacturing process. These individuals must be able to get along with others and have much experience on the equipment that you will be using to manufacture your products. You will also need equipment suppliers who will give you technical information, support, set up the equipment, and train your personnel on how to operate this new equipment.

You will also need to secure a building that will house your manufacturing facility, keeping in mind that you must also be able to secure equipment, inventory, raw materials, office equipment, restroom facilities, employee break room facilities, and generally a safe environment for your production personnel.

The facility that you will choose must be zoned appropriately for what you intend to use it for. You will need to check with your city, county, or municipality to ensure the allowance and to secure the business permit that you will be required to have before you begin your processing.

SALESPERSON OR INNOVATOR

Most innovators would think that they are the best person to sell their innovation to others; however, this could be the furthest thing from the truth. The innovator would be smart, before they start the sales stage, to do an actual auto-analyzation to decide if they are the best person to sell or represent their innovation.

If you are not the person who will best represent or sell your innovation, stop and hire professionals that will. The damages that an innovator can cause to their innovation sometimes may be irreversible. This is not what you want for your innovation.

However, if you are comfortable in public, friendly, and have good communication skills, of course you would be the best person to represent your product. People like to purchase from innovators and like to get to know them if they are friendly.

If you would still like to be involved with the sales process, take courses that will teach you how to sell. If you have communication problems, you can seek help from the likes of ToastMasters.com. They meet in a group setting and help with public speaking, leadership, and communications. Again, any innovator who plans to succeed needs to educate themselves even on the art of selling, which requires good speaking skills. Don't try to take shortcuts, for you will pay the price.

I've known of cases where the innovator is called—by his own family and employees—"the anti-sales department"! This is an example of what *not* to become. Needless to say, this innovator lost all of his sales team, never again to be recovered. On the bright side, after the heart attack that this innovator had suffered, this writer's son reconsidered and decided to help him on the design stage, and also to fix his existing molds. His new design was a success and his new molds worked much more efficiently. His health stabilized and he is much happier these days. He also decided to retire and is enjoying his golden years.

Yes, innovation can bring the good, bad, and the ugly out of each and every one of us. Before you take a step forward, make sure that you are stepping into solid ground that won't give out under your weight. If we overestimate our abilities, the person that we will be hurting the most is ourselves. In the words of John Green, "It hurts because it matters."

The takeaway is to never, never, never, represent or sell for yourself or your innovation, if there is a better professional who can do it for you. Andrew Carnegie said, "The secret of success lies not in doing your own work but in recognizing the best person to do it." Now, if one of the richest men in the world during his lifetime said this, it would be very smart advice to follow.

REACHING THE MATURITY STAGE

Any innovator that has come as far as to have a sales team network and have its own factory facility has more than likely reached the mature business stage. More than likely, you are in it for the long term. Your customer base network is now consistently purchasing your products, and the customers appear to be purchasing consistently.

During this stage, your business is now possibly turning a healthy profit and things are going smoothly. When you reach this stage, there will be some questions like, "Where do we go from here?" One possible direction will be whether you continue to risk and budget on additional innovation or whether you increase the marketing budgets to continue to grow current business levels.

The innovator with this decision to make will have some hard decisions to make and would be smart to seek all the information, if it has not been done yet, on what kind of market size they are in and what kind of market share they currently hold. This information must be provided by a company that specializes in providing it, specifically in market size. This will be expensive; however, it will help you strategize and navigate the future of the business in a very smart way. They say that "information is power." This is one of those moments where it is so true. The innovator will be smart to go over the acquired information and become very familiar with it.

Again, this information is the guide to take the company into the future. If the budgets for marketing and advertising are increased and that's the final decision, it could mean additional growth for the company; however, there is no guarantee of this. The reason for this may be twofold. One, the market may already be aware of your innovation and your innovation may be matured already, therefore no substantial new business may come from the increased advertising budgets. And two, the competition may be taking a hold of some of the market and similar product may have caught up to the innovator's product.

If the decision is made that the budgets will be increased for new innovation, this could mean that if the new innovation is a hit, the company will benefit from this and possibly distance itself from the competition. However, this may come with even more risk than increasing the advertising!

Once the decision has been made, the plan will be carried out and the innovator will have to live with his or her decision. There is a downside: if a new innovation that is introduced to the industry does not succeed, all the competitors will be watching and gauging its success or failure. With increased advertising, the only downside would be a low or no return for the company's added investment. However, one bright side of advertising is that there is no way for your competitor to monitor or gauge whether the company succeeded or failed.

If the innovator's business has reached the maturity level, they will most certainly be faced with government regulation. Government regulation comes in different forms. The biggest and most challenging of these regulations is taxes. All innovators must be aware that as soon as their business has become profitable, it is not uncommon that a combined yearly percentage of the profits of 50% is due. This combination consists of state, federal and local taxation. The business needs to have good cash flow to cover this expense. The last thing you need is to not pay these taxes, for the penalties and interest can become very expensive if left unpaid. The government also has the power of taking over any business that does not pay its taxes. On top of this, those who do not pay the taxes can also face charges of tax evasion, which carries criminal charges and possible imprisonment.

The taxing authorities will always be suspicious of any business that is growing exponentially. They may look at your tax forms and call you to question you about your filing. If the questioning goes wrong or the agent is still suspicious, they can order what is called a tax audit. Tax audits can take multiple years to resolve. If you are faced with this situation you may have to hire a tax attorney that will represent you. All innovators with year-over-year solid sales growth would be wise to hire an accountant to help with all the financials and to prepare all the tax filings in an orderly and timely manner.

THE FIRST COMPETITOR STRIKES

If your business has not been affected by a competitor yet, you have been very fortunate so far. This is called the "blue ocean effect," where the waters are clear of predators. When the competitors first appear, the waters will turn from blue to red. A red ocean means that there will be blood in the water as competition increases.

We have already covered the risk/reward effect that can come from either a failed or a successful new innovation. Again, if the innovation is a hit, it has the potential of keeping your business in the blue ocean effect, regardless of competition. That is a huge reward and many innovators risk it all to navigate their businesses in these waters. This is the ideal situation that any innovator would be wise to seek and to strive for.

If your new innovation is a bust, you will soon be aware of this. At this point, you will need to make counter-adjustments quickly, so as to keep distance between you and the competition. But how do you do this? One suggestion is to double down and innovate a new innovation.

Warning! This can become a risk of huge proportions! For if you do not succeed the second time around, it is possible that debt would be piled up to the point of you having to close the doors due to going out of business. So this may not be the higher risk that you want to take.

A story that comes to this writer's mind is that of an innovator who had come up with the idea for the first Mexican buffet lunch. The innovator quickly grew his existing operation with his new concept as the new business model proved to be a success! The innovator found himself within the blue ocean effect. These were wonderful times for him and his organization. The innovative idea became so successful that the innovator eventually ended up with a total of four locations.

However, the competition began to strike at his new concept and opened up a new location close to his most successful store. What a disappointment! The innovator, not having planned for this and not being totally prepared for this kind of growth, soon began to make business mistakes. One of the first mistakes that he made was to stretch out his existing team and require them to work many more extra hours. This left the team tired and in disarray. Meanwhile, his competition continued to eat at his business. Yes, indeed, the red ocean effect had arrived! Another big mistake that the innovator made was that he began to argue about the lease agreement conditions with one of the landlords. What made this a worse mistake was that this landlord owned the innovator's biggest and most successful location. This prompted a lawsuit that eventually took that location into Chapter 7 bankruptcy. This is the type of bankruptcy where all is lost. The time, money, and energy consumed by the innovator was huge. He began to lose so much focus that he ended up losing the other two locations that he had also previously opened. He was back to square one and was only left with his original location. However, he had compiled such a huge amount of debt that he had to file personal bankruptcy. The innovator began to experience the effects that come with failed planning, even though his innovation concept had been a big success. The failure had come with lost life savings, his health began to fail, his marriage began to fail, and key employees he had always depended on were no longer there.

But this is not all! The innovator was not down and out yet. You see, he was a fighter and had been a fighter since he was a young boy, he would not give up that easy!

So, one day, I got a call from the innovator. We were close, so he liked to hear my point of view. I was really surprised to hear from him at this point. What was also interesting is that he made the call very early in the morning. As I answered the phone, he greeted me and we exchanged niceties. I was in shock when he told me that he was thinking of taking one more big risk! To my dismay, he explained to me that there was added opportunity and that he was thinking of taking a final big risk. He explained it as, "I'm thinking of rolling the dice again." It sounded like he thought he was in Las Vegas and that he was in a simple game of shooting dice. He was clearly not realizing how another failed attempt could potentially put him down and out—and this time for good! I asked him the tough questions, like, "How did you get yourself into this predicament?: He told me what happened to him and his business, but all the time, it seemed to me like he was minimizing the gravity of the situation.

Knowing him well, I knew what he wanted to hear from me. He wanted to hear that, sure, he should just go for it. However, he never got another shot at the opportunity. His health worsened faster as his last location continued to suffer from the combined effect of a big load of debt and competition.

The innovator passed away, never to recover! After his family buried him they were forced to close the original location that had taken two generations to build up—50 years of blood, sweat and tears. It was a very sad day for all who knew him. The takeaway of the story is beware of taking risk, you must control the urge when starting your journey to success. Be patient and plan well before you travel!

INNOVATOR OR GAMBLER?

As already discussed, every innovator must decide whether they are going to take the risk of innovating or not. It's one thing to think that someday into the future you would like to innovate. It's another thing to say, I'm going to risk it all, and I want it now!

But what creates this mentality of looking for quick satisfaction? What could possibly make anyone be willing to risk it all?

Different factors can contribute to this. Some of these are the following:

1. Denial
2. Delusion
3. Madness
4. Unreasonableness
5. Fallacy

We will discuss each of these conditions that an innovator must watch out for, like a physician would watch for a disease! As an innovator, you must be constantly vigilant that you do not fall into any of these conditions. If you do, you must react quickly to get rid of them, for being afflicted with any one of them will put you down and out for the count. These type of conditions ruin people, communities, and even entire countries.

Denial – This is a condition that infects and clouds the thinking process and that creates a sense of stubbornness and seeing things differently, without confirmation. The innovators afflicted by this can see reality starring straight into their face, but in their minds, it looks like something rosier, and they expect a different outcome regardless of the warning bells signaling otherwise. When the eventual outcome is ruin, the innovator afflicted by this condition will believe that there are still many options left.

Delusion – This is a condition that also afflicts the thinking process and that creates a sense of refusing to believe information that has been presented, especially if this information goes against the innovator's planning and what they believe or think that the future will be. The condition is also associated with the innovator seeing things or hearing things that are not so. Paranoia is usually something that will follow delusion.

Madness – This is a condition that not only affects the mental thought process negatively, but also the physical wellbeing of the innovator. When madness sets in, all hope is lost and the best way to approach this condition, for those not afflicted, is to avoid anyone with this condition altogether. Madness is guaranteed to lead the innovator and all those around them into certain ruin.

Unreasonableness – This is a condition that affects the mental thought process and creates thoughts of grandiosity. This condition comes associated with feelings that anything can be accomplished, regardless of the challenge or difficulty. The innovator with this condition becomes more and more difficult to work with. This is usually associated with impossible goals being set by the innovator, regardless of the difficulty.

Fallacy – This is a condition that affects the point of view and comes associated with mistaken beliefs. This condition is also associated and based on unsound argument. This then becomes an innovator's mindset—that just because they believe a certain thing, this is the way it must be, especially if the information is given by people that they admire.

The innovator with any of the abovementioned conditions will certainly begin to make decisions like a gambler, and not a well-prepared innovator. Again, this will surely lead any innovator into ruin!

Innovators must always avoid having a gambler's mentality, for the journey to success and all the roads that lead to it are lined with countless carcasses that took risks just like a gambler would—and ended up being just another victim and a big loser. But how does the innovator avoid risking it all, just like a gambler would? You have to plan, strategize, budget, know your entry point as well as your exit plan. Only then will you be unlike a gambler. You will not take risk that is unreasonable to take, period. You will then be positioned to win, as the odds will be stacked up in your favor.

INNOVATOR OR HYENA?

There are many kinds of people who profess to be innovators. This type of wannabe innovator is only an "idea person". They love pitching their idea to friends and family, only shooting from the hip, yet have nothing to show for it. The "idea person" does not spend money on their own ideas, designs, prototypes, etc. The reason for this is that they are trying to persuade others to buy into their idea so they can sell it and be compensated by the buyer. They try to convince any person who will listen to them—mostly family and friends—that their idea would be a good investment and would be a smart approach to anyone trying to establish good economic situation for themselves.

These self-proclaimed innovators are always trying to feed off of others' kill. They prefer to steal from others rather than work on their own idea. If approached and asked why they decide to operate this way, they will respond that they are "idea people" first and foremost, and that they create opportunity for others. It is not unlikely for these so-called "idea people" to have a whole myriad of ideas floating around their heads at all times. They are not willing to invest or risk their own time, money and energy, doing the diligence that is required, on their own ideas.

This writer compares these so called "idea people" to the hyena. The hyena is a very interesting wild animal that roams around in the African safari. Hyenas are predators and are some of the savviest carnivores. They do not have many predators that can prey on them. Most hyenas are only killed by lions, and this is due to battles over prey. So, the next time you are approached by an "idea person," use caution, as these are very savvy predators like the hyena and will try to prey on you when you least expect it.

Any innovator would be wise to not disclose their innovation, but instead keep it guarded. "Idea people" do not value their ideas much, so they are quick to talk about them, as they are looking to make a quick buck and will quickly move to another venture or idea within hours or days. This is the kind of world that they live in. So an innovator should choose whether they will be a true innovator who plans, budgets, and strategizes, or be like the proverbial hyena, never creating value for themselves and those around them, lazy, and preferring to always trying to steal from others instead of hunting for their own food. What an ugly life that can lead to—a life full of dissatisfaction, anxiety, and unhappiness.

COMPETITION FORCES INNOVATION

The writer has always noticed that, throughout history, our capitalist system in the U.S. fosters competition and innovation. This is the very thing that allowed our system to flourish, and therefore facilitated our country to become the industrial powerhouse it is now. This only happened in a matter of 200 years!

When competition is fostered, innovation moves quickly—sometimes at a violent pace, leaving those that are not innovating adrift in the ocean and facing a sure death of either drowning or being eaten alive by sharks. Sometimes business owners relax with their innovation, and when they least expect it, the competition strikes back with a new version of their innovation. It is during these types of moments that an entrepreneur must choose to stand still and hold the line and see how things play out, or act quickly, playing in a more reactionary way.

Not quickly reacting sometimes can have very adverse effects. It may allow the competition to erode your market share, exposing your business model and possibly dealing a death blow to your innovation, your organization and eventually your business. This has the potential to happen very quickly. So if you have decided to toe the line just as a competitor brings a new innovation into the marketplace, you must keep this in mind. You will need to closely monitor the situation and then, if you begin to take some on serious damage, you must react quickly.

Some entrepreneurs may ask, "How do I do this if I do not have the resources now?" Well, you need to consider whether to sell, partner up or merge with a company that is capable of taking the hit and that can fight back. Or you can decide to walk away from it all and close your business's doors. Neither choice sounds very good, as you more than likely started to innovate because you wanted to start a company from your innovation, and then see it through and possibly, eventually, hand off your company to your offspring.

Any entrepreneur, when faced with this type of situation, must be sure that whatever move they make, it will be based on accurate data and not on just gut feelings. Therefore, entrepreneurs must never wait until competition strikes, as most of the time it will be too late and the game may be over. Therefore, constant budgeting for further future innovation must always be part of any sensible business plan. The goal for innovation is to continue and extend the time period in which your innovation leads the field. Only then will you be sailing in blue oceans and benefit from the blue ocean effect.

BEWARE, FOR THE COMPETITION MAY SET TRAPS

Beware! If not careful, an innovator may find themselves caught in what this writer calls an "innovator's spiral." This is a downward spiral that takes and ruins everything in its way, much like a tornado, only leaving death and destruction in its aftermath. Many times, the competitors that begin to innovate or even purchase others' innovations, can also run the danger of getting caught up in in their own trap and can also be swept away into their own destruction.

There are different ways that the competition purposely sets up these traps. Many times, the trap is years in the making and will begin to take a more businesslike feel. This can be like purchasing another company in the space with its own intellectual property. At first, this looks like a normal transaction; however, it may have a more sinister purpose. The transaction may sometimes be a forced transaction, but when this is the case, most of the time the purchasing company will require that the seller sign an NDA, or non-disclosure agreement. Therefore, it is difficult, even after the fact, to know about any sinister motives committed by the buyer. A very dangerous trap may be set up by the competitor once they are armed with intellectual property that they just purchased—they may then combine it with their existing intellectual property.

When any innovator becomes aware of these type of purchases among competitors within the same space, they would be wise to consult with professionals. Instead of rushing into just making the next improvement to their innovation, a novice innovator may not be aware that they may be running into a field full of land mines. If this were to happen, they would surely get cut down and possibly face certain death from the mortal wounds this situation could pose. The reason for this is that the combined intellectual property now held by the competition might be so broad that it could be impossible to navigate legally without infringing on their property. If any innovator finds themselves in this situation for lack of planning or lack of experience, it can mean the end of their innovation run within this space. However, any innovator that still decides to move ahead, regardless of the risks, may find themselves faced with a lawsuit. This always brings dire consequences. It will mean countless hours of legal issues to be addressed by the innovator, many assets diverted for legal costs, court appearances, and the many other headaches associated with being in a lawsuit.

On the same token, any competitor that combines intellectual property and uses it to stifle others' innovation by suing may find themselves in the crossfire of litigation. Unfortunately, once these types of proceedings start, it may take years for both parties to end up settling or for the courts to make the final decisions. By this time, millions of dollars have been spent, and both companies will be exhausted.

Many times, lawsuits tend to change the face of the players involved. Some competitors can end up being forced to sell their business in order to pay their legal bills. Other competitors may end up having to file bankruptcy in order to survive. The thing about lawsuits is that there are usually no winners—in fact, the winners may become other companies that may take advantage of the situation and purchase either competitor at a substantial discount.

UNDERHANDED COMPETITOR TACTICS

Many intellectual property lawsuits, especially among competitors, are complex and may require legal review. An innovator faced with this situation would be smart to consult with legal counsel. Legal counsel may conclude, after hearing and understanding the current situation, that there is enough to serve a lawsuit for the violation of current antitrust and monopoly laws.

Whether the competition is aware or not makes no difference with antitrust or monopoly laws. The competition may have committed an illegal act by purchasing others' intellectual property, combining it with their existing property, and then launching a lawsuit against your current innovation. Again, these are very complex issues that only legal counsel can help you with. The time may come where these issues may have to be brought up in a court of law, where all of them will be discovered and discussed. The innovator requesting relief by the court may get it, and it would be smart to request that its competitor be tied to a code of conduct approved by the court moving forward.

This does not necessarily mean that all the competitor's attacks will stop. It is possible that much of your advertising and marketing materials will be put in question in front of a court. Again, this is a tactic to foster fear and to stymie any kind of advance that your company is making over the competition. These attacks can come at vulnerable times and are very violent. They are also expensive, take much effort to defend, and take much time. However, unlike other lawsuits, these types of lawsuits have to be defended at all cost, or your company's message will surely forever be altered, and you may be left with an ineffective message. If you give in and simply fold to your competition, they will be glad to make your message bland, especially if it contains benefits that the competing product does not have.

Yes, the journey to success is full of traps, predators, cannibals, and if you are not watchful you will either lie hostage or be eaten alive, and your carcass will be left for the wild animals to finish off. Do not become a victim—become a victorious innovator.

Later in the book, we will cover ways in which this could be done even if you are currently a small competitor. Size does not always matter; this challenge can be overcome by using strategy before moving forward with your next innovation. You must always plan for the future and get the market entry point just right when you are making an attempt to move the market your way. There are no shortcuts to going about this. If you find out that you are not ready and the timing is off, immediately put the brakes on your plan. You must then plan to gear up with what you presently lack and prepare for the future.

Disaster's Aftermath

Much like in the aftermath of a tornado, the landscape after a disaster dramatically changes. It changes when other companies get into the space and as new players begin to compete for their market share. What creates an even more competitive environment is that these companies are bigger, stronger, and have more products to offer your customers, and at lower prices. At this point, this is called the "red ocean effect." The waters become full of blood as prices get dropped aggressively. Then additional discounts are offered on what these companies refer to as "bundling." Bundling is when you, as the buyer, purchase more lines and you receive more of a discount. The problem with those kinds of deals is that smaller competitors don't stand a chance.

If your business is faced with this kind of competitive situation, you will have no choice but to offer added discounts to match the competition's pricing, or have lower pricing altogether. However, the only way to accomplish this is to improve the way that you currently manufacture your product or streamline. This can be accomplished by the use of automation, which can many times improve the quality of your product, leaving you with an additional feature if your new automated product is superior in quality to the competition's.

If you streamline, you may have to cut your payroll budgets, marketing budgets, advertising budgets, lower your inventory levels, etc. There is risk in cutting either or all of the abovementioned things. However, the benefits outweigh the risks. If you do not respond with lowered pricing at the right time, many of your current customers will be tempted to purchase from your competitor. This will leave your company vulnerable and weak to other attacks. It may eventually fall due to a decline in sales, demoralized employees, frustrated vendors, etc.

The positive effects of downsizing and streamlining can bring countless benefits and insight in improved profits, leaner meaner employees, happy vendors, etc.

If you are one of the lucky surviving innovators, once the tornado is done, there will be time to rebuild. This will take hard work, and it is common for the rebuilding process to take many years to be accomplished.

As the years go by, and you, the innovator, begin to rebuild and feel the positive effect of not being in a long and arduous war, the wounds will begin to heal, and you will be armed with much more experience. You will also get the respect of many by being recognized as a war hero and survivor. As the rebuilding takes place, you will then be able to plan and contemplate the future. It's possible that you may be ready to move on and sell your business or pass your business on to your offspring. If this is the case, this writer congratulates you, hoping that you were able to save some money along the away during your journey to success. This writer wishes that every successful innovator enjoys their retirement, with enough resources to do the things that they always dreamed of doing, or go to the places that they always dreamed of going to. This has to be the goal of each innovator, otherwise what's the use of all the effort and blood, sweat, and tears?

Unfortunately, the history books are full of stories with innovators who accomplished great feats, only to eventually end up in despair, ruin, suicide, and self-destruction. Innovation does not have to be a dirty word; however, just the mention or the attempt of becoming an innovator brings chills to many, as this is so commonly associated with high risk. The stories that derive from the past leave a long trial of shattered and broken dreams. Many families have also suffered from the negative effects of the high risk that is associated with the process of innovation. Innovation can mean the difference between success and failure and therefore can be very enticing for those that are suffering from economic distress.

If you have decided that you will continue to lead your business, this writer recommends that you, the businessperson, put on their innovator cap once again, as you may well be wanting to regrow your business and get it back to a long-term growth trajectory.

Mentoring the Art of Innovation

In the last chapter, we covered the need to go back and begin to innovate if you are in it for the long term, especially now that more time has passed since you have innovated, and especially now that your business has survived countless assaults by a larger, predatory competitor. Your business has finally arrived at a peaceful juncture and innovation is what will spark the next spurt of growth. You might be asking yourself, "Well, where do I start?" Many businesspeople would probably feel pretty exhausted by now, so the last thing they are looking to do is to go back right away and begin to innovate again. What may be a good idea is to take a break—possibly take a nice vacation and relax. Once you're back and well relaxed, you will be able to think much more clearly and plan much better. If you are still not feeling like getting back into the innovation process, there may be some options.

Sometimes an innovator feels like the only person that can do the job is them. So many times, innovation can get postponed or pushed back due to this. This is a big mistake for any company, when instead the innovator can simply pick one or several of its most loyal employees and form a team that can further innovation so that the weight of the process does not fall on only one person. However, this will take mentoring. Mentoring means to advise or train someone, especially a younger colleague. All innovators must have the patience to foster this kind of growth, especially if your goal is to keep your company for the long term. If you find that you are not in the situation to mentor, or that you just don't trust anyone with this, then it may be time to sell your company, or just cruise and not come up with any new innovations and continue to prolong the life of your business as long as you can.

The mentoring process can be full of challenges, as it may be hard to get a meeting of the minds with multiple individuals when it comes to issues like deciding what design looks better, which design will work better, what design has the best chance of success, etc. The process, with multiple persons working on it, can also be challenging due to age differences as well. No one said that innovation is easy; however, if you and your team hit a home run with your new innovation, it will be so satisfying that you may all be looking for a repeat. However, if this is the case, stop, take a break, and enjoy the moment, because they can be few and far between. Do not think that you are guaranteed the next big winner. Always remember you must plan, just like NASA plans every trip into space with the proper amount of fuel, personnel, equipment, supplies, and destination approach. Likewise, you must plan for the next stage of business growth. But just because you have experienced a certain amount of success, it does not mean that you should stop strategizing and planning.

If you are willing to mentor, innovation mentoring takes time and does not come automatically. The person or persons that you will be mentoring will have to get ground-floor training and experience, and many time hands-on experience, as only this will give them the confidence to eventually become innovators themselves—and the knowledge required to communicate with a team about design, solutions, ideas and or proposals.

This writer has been in the difficult situation of wanting to innovate but not being sure on design, efficiency, material processing, etc. So, since his older son had just received his master molder certificate in one of the most respected schools in the world and had worked for the family business for approximately 10 years, he felt like his son might be a good candidate to mentor to begin innovating. The writer proceeded to reach out to his son about a new idea that he was thinking of developing into an innovation. As they started conversing, the issues came up about whether the material processing was even possible on this new proposed innovation. After a thorough analysis, the son came back with the good news that the material processing would work—and that the design would allow the material process to work quite well. So, they got to work together on a design, and then they both moved into the prototype stage. After a few adjustments, the product was ready to be shown. They took the product to a local tradeshow and it was a huge success! They hit the proverbial home run: the innovation continues to sell well and is now producing millions of dollars in added revenue.

While this sounds easy, it was not! The reason is that it took 10 years of experience for the writer's son to gain the knowledge and grow technically. It also took the writer some patience. The outcome was successful. So if you have the stomach for this, then you should be able to accomplish the same. However, as a reminder, you will need to be patient.

COMPETITORS IN THE MIDST

So you have achieved a certain measure of success, and you are now noticed throughout the industry and even admired by many. You have earned respect and admiration, and that was also more than likely one of your motivations for becoming an innovator. So congratulations to you! Once again, this writer salutes you and applauds you and all your accomplishments, as you have now reached a place few can get to. You more than likely are at the stage where you are admired by your family, as they are proud to be recognized as the family member of a successful innovator in the community. Your friends salute you, and life is good.

However, competitors are always watching, and many times desire just what you have built. Their thought process, especially if they are a bigger company, is that your company may be a great complement, fit, and add-on to their current family of companies and products. There may be a time where they will contact you and ask for a meeting to consider a possible sale of your company. You may be interested in this at this time; even if not interested, it is always smart to make friends and to at least hear them out.

When the meeting comes, you must be alert, rested, and prepared. You will be asked questions about you and the company. You do not have to answer anything that you don't feel comfortable answering. The questions will be like, what are your yearly sales, how is the company doing financially, who are its other competitors, what amount of money you are looking to sell the company for, etc.

If you are prepared to move forward into a sale, more meetings will be set up as a follow-up and to settle into a sales agreement. Sometimes larger companies need to get board approval, and this can take some extra time. If all the indicators show that the buyer is still interested in the purchase of your company and has gotten board approval, then some of the remaining and final decisions will need to be made. Among these is a sales price for your company that you will accept. A good rule of thumb is a willing buyer and a willing seller is what creates a sale. It is more than likely that you will be offered a low price that you will not accept. However, you may be offered another, higher offer after the original offer. This may be more attractive to you, and you might accept. There is also another very important decision, and this is that many companies will try to put the owners on a three-year earn plan. This means that the final price of the sale would be paid depending on the performance of the three-year period. So there are some decisions for every business owner must decide.

Another decision is whether you want to remain for three years, or if you want to leave upon the sale of the business. All these are important issues that only you and your family can decide. You can always hire a business consultant or legal counsel that specializes in business sales for further information, as every business sale is different and some of these agreements come tied with non-compete clauses, non-disclosure clauses, etc.

A sale will require much disclosure, so be ready to present all this, as this process may take weeks or even months to be finalized. If you do decide to carry on with the sale of your company, this writer congratulates you and salutes you for a job well done. Always remember to be a force for good, and make sure that you always use the proceeds of your sale for good things and never for bad!

INFORMATION REQUEST

Some companies may purposely act as if they are asking for your company's information to further the purchase process, when they are in fact trying to secure inside information that they would otherwise not have access to. You may be fine with added exchange, as you do not see this company as a competitor since they do not work in your space.

When you are considering a possible sale of your company, make sure that if the initial price offer is not where you want it to be, the best thing to do is to stop sending information immediately. Competitors sometimes have the intent of using your company to gain customers as they position to begin to compete against you. Now armed with your customer list and your customer pricing programs, they are well-equipped to begin the process of picking your customers off one by one.

The red ocean effect is ugly, dirty, and bloody. It is not uncommon that once both parties have cooled off and backed away from the sales process, the same company who is presently known as a non-competitor brings out its own innovation and begins competing against you. Much to your dismay, you are in shock and regret that you handed over the information that you did. However, blinded by the promise of receiving millions of dollars for your company, you handed over everything that they ask for. This is a classic tactic, and you must be careful to guard against it.

So when the new competitor begins to tout its innovation, saying they will offer better pricing and more than likely bundle the new innovation with a discounted package so it may be purchased along with other products that they already offer. This will put added pressure on your customers to begin to purchase the competitor's new innovation. Hopefully your company finds itself with the ability to respond either by pricing promotion, the market favors your innovation to the point where any other competing innovation would be rejected, or your company has plenty of goodwill because of its superb excellent service and you have a solid customer base. It's kind of the Coca-Cola effect—substitutes will not cut it..

If your company can respond to the latest assault, then you are well positioned and have a bright future ahead of you. Few companies find themselves with this kind of enviable advantage. Consider yourself fortunate: now you have the credentials not just as good innovator, but a great innovator! Congratulations!

You now have the advantage of playing the long game, unlike many innovators who have tried and failed before you. This will now allow you not only to keep innovating into the future and improve your business skills, but also to transform your life as a self-innovation. It does not matter who we are or how well we do in life, there is always room for self-innovation, and self-improvement.

PLAYING THE LONG GAME

Again, it is highly unlikely that a small innovator will reach the top of the innovation apex with any of their innovations, as only 5 percent of these become commercially successful. The chances of becoming a one-hit wonder seem very possible. As with any highly popular song, the band or group that performs it is often referred to as a one-hit wonder if they are successful only once and cannot repeat the success the second time around.

If you do not want to be referred to as a one-hit wonder, even if no one around you is referring to you as such, it is normal to want to try and repeat the success for a second time. However, you will need to be in a place where few have gone. Most innovators may not be ready for that journey. The possibilities of having discord and disarray in your organization because of innovation is very much a possibility. Innovation can paralyze companies as the progress takes place; therefore, much secrecy needs to be used even within the organization. The innovation process may take convincing of others to design the innovation the way you are asking them to. It will also take others in your organization to be willing to support you while you take on more debt; we have already mentioned that many times unsuccessful innovation can ruin companies.

Also, a very important department is the sales department. The sales department will more than likely have to be consulted to consider whether the innovation would have a chance to succeed in the marketplace. You will be wise to have your sales department onboard before proceeding. The risks are high risk, but there's also high reward! If you can get your organization behind it, this means that your whole organization is taking a leap of faith and is hoping that the new innovation will be a smashing success.

The thing about innovation is that it gives us the possibility of setting ourselves free. What this means is that your innovation does not necessarily have to be in the same industry. Your innovation can find itself in an industry that is similar, but not the same. If your current competitors are not in this space, you might have a shot at experiencing a blue ocean effect. The only other challenge is that your innovation has to still become a smashing success.

If you proceed with this innovation and it does belong in another industry, you will more than likely have to start a new company altogether. This means that you will have to find a new locale and hire a new team to help you build the company from scratch. The genius of this is that if your innovation process is similar to your other innovations, you can have your original company supply your new company. You can use your same labor, equipment, and sometimes sales personnel at least for starters. This will help you a great deal logistically. This is what some businesspeople refer to as making lemonade.

SUCCESS STRIKES AGAIN

Again, your new innovation is a success! Lightning strikes twice! Congratulations and job well done! Now let's roll up our sleeves and go to work!

The road to success has been well planned and traveled already by you; you are now a veteran and know how to navigate dangerous terrain. You now have the experience to take on bigger responsibilities and to help change lives. Maybe this is a special calling for you or maybe not; however, just the fact that you are hiring more people and employing more personnel means that you are already part of the process of changing people's lives.

Steady employment can make a big difference to a child who cannot even think straight in school because they are thinking of their economic distress that their family is in. This has been proven to affect children in a very bad way, as they cannot concentrate in school and their learning process begins to fall behind their peers. Is it a wonder that we have so many individuals stuck in the cycle of crime, drugs and prostitution, among other things?

You, the successful innovator, can make a difference and help those in need, especially with the children, who become the biggest victims. As your new innovation continues to prosper, you will experience the compounding effect of success like you never have before. Again, few innovators ever get to this level of success and find themselves in a position to help others by changing lives in a positive way. The innovator that is a "force for good" will always find satisfaction in life.

By doing this, you will always guarantee having the reputation of being someone who helps others, and as the saying goes, "You reap what you sow." What this means is that if you sow a lemon seed and this seed grows to the point of becoming a fruit-bearing tree, you will be guaranteed to pick or reap lemons—not oranges, not peaches, just lemons. In other words. expect others to give you back what you give out. Monetary help is not the only way that an innovator can help others. The mentoring effect is something that can be done; as a very wise saying goes "Give a man a fish and you feed him for a day, show him how to fish and you feed him for a lifetime." Yes, indeed, helping and mentoring others ensures that they possess the knowledge and the tools that they will need to navigate the future, therefore securing economic security for a lifetime for themselves.

Many times, we can find ourselves wanting to help strangers only to find out that our own family members may be in need of economic help themselves. Another wise saying is, "Charity begins at home." This means that instead of helping others, we need to start with helping our own family first. Then, once that we have covered, we can help others.

BEING SELECTIVE

Being selective about who you mentor is a good idea. The fact that many people will want to learn from you or be mentored by you means that you will have to be highly selective, as you do not want your time to be wasted on someone who really does not want to learn and does not have the dedication or the drive. There are those individuals that seek the so-called "freshly caught fish" already caught, and still expect a daily handout. They prefer not to learn to fish. For sure, these are not individuals that you would want to mentor. You ultimately want to mentor individuals with qualities who show a deep interest in learning, who demonstrate a high degree of dedication, and who will truly appreciate having been given the opportunity to be trained in the art of innovation.

Your mentoring has much value; therefore, it is to be held as such. The individual selected to be your protege is someone who will want to share in and eventually mentor others. These are the individuals that you must want to invest in, as they will be instrumental into the future of your organization and you will also need personnel who you can trust. In the future, or when you are ready to slow down, these individuals should be ready to run your company on a daily basis, with little to no supervision. However, the innovation mentoring process will no doubt take years to begin to bear fruit. So get started as soon as possible.

The new innovation will take a period of studying and testing from you, the innovator. You will no doubt have to immerse yourself in the new subject matter—identifying the problem and how to solve it. This will take a considerable amount of time and it is not uncommon for new innovations to require years of study, which entail long periods of reading, researching, isolation, concentration, designing, prototyping and, finally, testing.

This is the time where much frustration and patience will be required by the innovator. If any of these items is rushed or skipped, it is more than likely that this will come back to bite you and that the innovation will have a good chance of failure. There are no shortcuts; this is one of the main reasons why many businesspeople avoid innovation at all cost.

The individual or individuals chosen for this process will without a doubt be instrumental to your undertaking. This period will be a period of much professional growth for your protege, and this will become invaluable for your whole organization. Once you are done with the innovation process and are ready to start the introduction process, you will need to get your marketing, graphics, and sales departments on board to start planning for the message that will accomplish the best way of presenting the innovation.

Marketing a New Innovation

The method of marketing a new innovation can at times be difficult for the simple reason that maybe the problem that the innovation solves has not yet been identified by the industry. It is possible that the marketing will have to mention the problem and then the solution. This, of course, will take educating the industry and much more time, effort, and expense will have to take place. However, if executed quickly and well, the chance of dominating that space will be very possible. The sales department will have to work diligently to ensure that the space gets dominated as soon as possible. This will require many presentation meetings, training meetings, and much travel.

The budgets for all this will have to be reviewed, as this will not be a mature market that you are addressing, one that allows lowered marketing and advertising budgets. Again, you will have to go big with tradeshow planning, updating the booth graphics, creating the brochures required, etc.

The process will again be slow and arduous, as anything that is worthwhile cannot be built overnight. Again, this will require much patience and time, as the process will be a long hard slough before it begins to bear fruit. While in this process of planting, the innovator will be wise to refer back to the time when they first started to introduce their innovation into the marketplace. While it is true that some innovations become an instant success, most innovations take a while to be introduced, purchased, and then repurchased.

On the positive side, this will be a great time for your organization to spot good talent and to hire the new sales talent that the new innovation will need to continue to be sold. Numbers don't lie, and you want to make sure that success is measured and directly tied to results, and that politics doesn't become the very reason why a person is still employed regardless of lack luster results.

Because you can only project the numbers that you will be required to ship, you won't totally be sure how many units will actually be required and how soon; therefore, you will need to inventory some units so that availability will not become a problem in the first place. If shipping is not done in a timely manner, this has a tendency to discourage the sales team from pushing hard. You want to make sure that your production department makes and stocks plenty of inventory before any introduction begins. As the weeks and months go by, you will have a better idea of how much inventory you will be needing to always stay ahead of demand. Your goal should always be to ship all orders on the same day received, or at the latest, on the following day. This will ensure that all your customers get familiar with your new company and that they become confident that delivery will always be prompt.

Incubator Training

As a business grows, it is important that it begins to decentralize from the original innovator to other individuals in the organization. The reason for this is that the original innovator will be primarily involved with the day-to-day operations and the fine tuning of the business—or more than likely, by this time, *businesses*. There are several ways of integrating systems that will work and continue to foster new personnel. Many companies depend on training programs to foster the discovery of new potential talent before making any employee commitment.

The practice of internships has been a long and successful method that many companies integrate into their businesses in order to foster and recruit new talent. An internship program is not difficult to begin. You can simply spread the word with your family and employees, or post it on your website or in local college bulletins. The posting needs to have a brief description of what your company does, its location, and a summary of what the internship is all about. Individuals will then apply much like applying for employment.

Once you have selected certain individuals, you will start an interview process and decide which applicant would be better suited for the internship and which one will be the best fit within your organization. The agreement will be set and negotiated on the bases of hours required, schedule, and the project assignment. The pay will also be agreed upon; usually, this will be pay on a per-hour basis only. Internships are many times not paid as the experience gained to the student has inherent value. However, many companies pay the going minimum wage set by the state that you are located in. And you will find that students are more than happy with this kind of arrangement.

Before the student begins the internship they should be trained on what they will work on, which is usually a project that the company will have preset for interns. Companies usually advance the projects that their other employees don't have the time for. The internship program allows an individual or individuals to concentrate on these very projects. This will ensure fast progress. The internship program can be a win/win for all those involved. It also allows a company to test and try the new potential talent that it will be hiring once the student graduates from the college or university they are attending.

This will create a pipeline and will ensure a constant flow of new potential talent that you may want to eventually employ. Internships allow a low-cost solution of extra talent to finalize current projects that will help the company grow, and at the same time get to try out some of the interns that may be interested in eventually becoming employed by the company. Therefore, internships are highly recommended for any company that is growing, as they allow it to have hiring options in the future.

It is always recommended that you hire only college graduates, as this can say a lot about the job candidate. This writer has had both good and not-so-good results when confronted with this issue of hiring. In the writer's experience, there was an exceptionally good result when he decided to offer his youngest son, who at the time was attending Boston University, an internship during his summer break.

The son accepted and got right to work. The project was about analyzing statistics for certain products that this writer was interested in innovating. The project also included the market size and the total sales potential. The son worked all summer long on this project and did a superb job. The writer offered his son a job to help run the company. The new innovation was also part of the responsibilities that the son would have, including growing the new innovation that the company decided to move forward on. The hire was a great idea, and showed a very successful result. This also allowed the son to get a feel for working at the company and gave him a glance as to what the potential was. Again, a great success story of how internships can go without a glitch.

However, sometimes it's easy for business owners to hire young employees that do not have college degrees and that just graduated from high school. The reason for this is that most of the time the young person has the advantage of being related or knowing one of the key employees. This hiring practice does not work the majority of the time. However, from time to time, you may be able to find a diamond in the rough. Just don't be surprised if there are many challenges before the diamond shines!

This writer knew a young man who was related to one of his vendors. The young man's father asked if he could possibly be given a chance at employment. He did disclose that his son was going through some tough personal times. The young man had just graduated from high school and was not attending college. This writer agreed to give this young man a chance of employment, even though it was not the hiring practice.

There is an interesting story behind this young man. After the young man started to work it became apparent that he was a fast learner; however, it also became apparent that he lacked discipline and motivation. The months passed by, and he was OK handling the customer department, which he kept going in a minimally satisfactory way. So he kept his job and started to "cruise," meaning that he did just enough to stay employed, but not more.

One day, one of his fellow employees brought an excited prospective customer to the office. This person was interested in finding out more about the product, as he had not seen the product yet, so the fellow employee asked the young employee if he could help explain the product since the young man was well-versed in the product line and was part of the customer service department. The young man did not reply and had a blank look in his face. His fellow employee told the prospective customer that maybe some brochures would do for now, which the prospective client agreed to take.

When the fellow employee reported the incident to the human resource department, it became apparent that there would have to be an investigation of this incident. It was later learned that the young man had just returned from his lunch break in which he had been smoking marijuana. Management quickly moved to put him on leave for the time being and sent him to counseling and therapy, including random drug testing. The young man agreed to it. However, he did not express much motivation in continuing with his recovery. At that, management decided to let him go. A very sad story indeed. However, that is not the end.

A few months later, the young man came back to the business and asked to speak with management. He said that he was sorry about his past behavior and that he would like to have his job back. The management responded that this was not going to be that easy. It reminded the young man that he had some serious issues that he needed to take care of—even before being considered for employment. He proceeded to mention that he had taken all the steps to correct his past issues and that he had hit rock bottom after he got fired. You see, when he went out of town with his friends, his car got towed after he parked it in some other person's assigned parking. After begging the police officers to release his vehicle, they told him that it was now out of their hands and that he had to deal with the towing company. The bigger problem was that he had spent all his money buying pot; therefore, he could not pull his car out of storage. So, not having any money and being out of town, he was desperate. He had really hit rock bottom, being broke and homeless at the same time. On top of his worries was the fact that both of his parents were out of the country.

This indeed was a moment that hit him very hard. He mentioned that he began to think of the time when this writer had told him to make sure to make his father proud, and that the only reason he had been given an employment opportunity was because of his father. The fact that his father was a good, hard-working man, and had made many sacrifices to give his son the opportunity to be born and grow up in America. Yes, he was the son of immigrants who came from the other side of the globe. As he told the story, his tears rolled down his face, giving a strong indication of sorrow, shame, and sincere repentance. He knew that he had failed his father and he claimed that he had made changes. He started by mentioning that he was totally clean and that he had found the power of prayer to help him. He also mentioned that he had stopped associating with all his friends, and that he had removed everything toxic from his life. He said that he was now willing to go into random drug testing, being sure that any testing would come out negative—meaning zero use of drugs.

After much thought and discussion, the management team decided to give him his job back, pending the results of a drug test. Days later, he came out clean and was given his job back. He also started working out, eating better and his personal grooming improved. He is now a happier person, even though he is still having to go through random drug testing now and into the future.

The reason why this writer felt that this young man's story was worth mentioning is that this young man was still very young. An experience like his had without a doubt left a big impression on him. However, the overarching thing that the management team considered was this young man's age, and how he was still very young. There was a very real possibility of being able to mold him into one day becoming a very valuable company asset, especially with all the life experience that he could someday share with other young people. Sometimes a bit of compassion can go a long way!

EMPLOYEE MORALE

Your company, or companies, by this time find themselves sailing along the cool waters of the blue ocean!

It is at this time that a review of the organization's benefit program is important. The last thing that any organization needs at this time is internal strife. So the employee benefit program should be reviewed, especially now that the time has come that the company is receiving multiple income streams from its innovations, which are now being sold in the marketplace. The profits are without a doubt doing well, and again, the company is within the blue ocean effect.

Any company owner can get nervous when the employee benefit program is about to be reviewed; this is only natural. However, it's always good to keep in mind that all the companies employees have been instrumental in making the company successful and will be needed to keep it successful for many years to come.

If you find that your current employee benefit program needs improvement, there are easy ways that will not cost much more money than what is currently being offered. Most companies have basic plans, and these depend on the size of your company. This usually include the following:

a. Paid holidays
b. Paid vacation
c. Employee appreciation luncheons
d. Health, dental, and vision care allowances

e. End of year party
f. End of year bonuses and recognition awards
g. Bonus programs tied to specific sales performance
h. Company credit cards
i. Paid-for gasoline
j. Royalty participation based on successful innovations
k. Company vehicle

Some companies have found out that luncheons are a good way for the organization to meet during business hours. They allow all the employees to eat together and socialize, and they are a good time for announcements on company progress and introductions of new hires, and they allow the ownership a chance to express its appreciation for all the hard work. If you offer your employees a similar benefit program, you are well on your way to having a happy and productive workforce. A benefit to the company is that these programs are fully tax deductible and will help any business lower its tax burden.

Innovators Higher Learning

It is recommended for any company owner or leader to continue to learn about the subject of business. As business is constantly evolving and changing. It is important to stay informed on all the new things that are going on, and to be able to network with likeminded business leaders. There are different forums that foster and allow this within their programs. These are sometimes multiple-week courses and are sponsored by business in association with leading business universities.

The participation in these high-caliber learning programs is many times by invitation only or requires sponsorship by others. If it's a program that has a high cost of participation, it usually takes an application process, along with an interview process. You will have to explain what you do and what size of organization you are currently running. There are usually preset criteria in order to qualify. If you are fortunate enough to be chosen, you will then be formally invited, and you will be well on your way to higher learning. You will more than likely have to travel to the university where the program is being held. Even though some of these programs are expensive, they will only require your travel and lodging expenses to be taken care of by you. Many of these programs include some meals as well; the cost of the sponsors can be up to $15,000 dollars per student. Again, these are high-caliber programs which include high-caliber speakers, and many times include the people who have worked for the big companies that are the most successful at the time.

The program includes participation, and the speakers talk about the different ways certain companies have succeeded. They many times share videos and interviews of the company founders. These conversations are sessions that are full of a wide array of subjects, like how to fund your company or ways on how to incentivize your employees, among many others.

The program may require that you go home and continue to work on a preset curriculum. This can take time and is usually six weeks long. You will need to send your work into the program on a weekly basis, and you will also be tested on all these subjects. You will need a passing grade in order to graduate. If all goes well and you have passed all the testing and participated in all of the curriculum—having also sent it back for review—you will then be notified that you have qualified to graduate. At the end of the course you will receive a certificate of completion and achievement.

Competition is always going to be looking for angles on how to overcome your business and, if possible, take it over. These learning programs will keep you positive and motivated. It's important to know and learn the inside scoop on how other successful leaders stay on the leading edge, regardless of the competition.

LEADERSHIP MORALE

Once you have worked on your employee morale, it is very important for you to continue to have confidence and self-esteem. In order to do this, you need to always have balance. This means that you need to allow time for yourself. There are individuals who never make time for themselves and end paying a deep price with premature illness and sometimes premature death. It is not uncommon for businesspeople to commit suicide as they lose their self-esteem and lose their confidence, especially when business goes back.

Allowing time for yourself will help to keep you in balance, so that whatever happens with the business, you will be better prepared to face what comes your way, regardless of what it is. Allowing time for yourself doesn't have to be costly or take a lot of time. If you like a sport like tennis or golf, these are two ideal ways to get away and could be very easy to add to your schedule. If you enjoy fishing or simply bird watching these may take a little longer time however not too much longer.

From time to time, it is advisable to take a vacation with your better half and enjoy the fruits of your hard work. This may be the right time to travel to other destinations in other parts of the world. These, ideally, would be places that you have always dreamed of visiting. You will find out that once you relax in this way, you will be eager to come back to work with a full charge to keep going. After all, most of us have started our businesses with this in mind. It's funny how we are eager to start our business to be able to one day be able to accomplish traveling to faraway places—and that sometimes, once this can be done, we invent a bunch of excuses of why it's a bad time to travel. If we are stuck in this mindset, that means that we are really in need of time off. If you don't feel like traveling ,you can simply take some time to hang around your house and read a book, do gardening, or simply finish a home project that you have been wanting to do for a long time.

Another suggestion that works for many businesspeople is scheduling spa massages. These come in a variety of choices like the hot rock massage, deep tissue massage, or arnica massage. These are all done as a therapeutic solution to relax the body and are offered at most resorts. You can also try the mineral bath springs; these are also therapeutic and are said to help the body heal up from aches, pains, arthritis and the like.

Whatever your situation may be, just leave the business for a few weeks and don't go back until some time has passed (more than likely a two-week period). After this, get ready and excited and go back to work. But if you still feel like you need a little more time then be sure to take it. You will feel the big difference.

You must now make this a goal as part of your new routine. But you may ask what's up with this? This sounds like a lot of wasted time! Believe me, this is time well invested in yourself. As we grow older, our bodies require more time to recover and the goal in doing this is not only to foster internal happiness but to gain longevity. This is priceless! We will go over other ways that you must consider as ways that you can gain longevity, happiness, a sense of well-being, and maybe even more productivity.

Stay Lean and Mean

Just like the whole business community strives to be lean and mean, so must you strive to be the same way. Being lean and mean when the phrase is applied to business it means "no fat or no extra fat." "Mean" is a benefit of being lean meaning quick, versatile, with much stamina, etc.

There are ways to help us become lean and mean. Usually the innovators who started their business a long time ago fall into patterns of overindulging, laziness, sloppiness in personal grooming, and even a bit sloppy with the dress code. There is sometimes room for improvement, fortunately, there are professionals who can help in these departments. We can talk about nice lofty goals on how we are going to improve in any one of these departments, but this may be more difficult than to make improvement in the business.

Making positive changes takes much discipline, motivation, and above all, hard work. When humans reach certain age, they can become creatures of habit. This means if we are used to drinking a six pack of beer daily, we will more than likely resent even the thought of having to give that up. If we are used to getting home and slouching on our sofas watching T.V., it is more than likely that we will not want to change this habit.

The changes that we are talking here are transformational, so unless your mind is ready to make the change, nothing else will do it—period. This means that we may need to get some professional counseling. Now, you may be thinking, "I am not crazy! I don't need to be talking to a shrink about my shortcomings." But keep in mind that it takes more courage to go to a professional in search of personal development than not doing anything at all. Again, you are after longevity and happiness. If you are not ready to consult with a professional, you can start by avoiding the people or the places that bring out this kind of behavior in us. There is a wise saying: "Who you surround yourself with you become." This may be good to keep in mind for starters, while you consider the value of consulting a professional.

When you have decided to move ahead with your transformation, you will find out that consulting with a professional can be very relaxing and can get you the advice that you may need to see your total transformation become a reality. The important thing to remember is that the mind can be very complex, and that you may have other challenges that make you do the things that will get in your way of transportation. Maybe you have depression or something else. Keep in mind that without our minds working properly, we will never be able to reach our goal of total transformation. Only professionals who have the expertise to diagnose any one of the conditions that may be afflicting us can help us with the treatments that will be needed in order to move forward.

Profit or Hobby

There are two types of innovators out there: the one who is profit driven and can't wait to improve his economic situation, and the other who only tinkers around hoping to have some kind of new breakthrough so that he can be called an inventor. These two types of innovators may sometimes get confused in their roles. On the one hand, the profit-driven innovator sometimes does not think before jumping into an idea, and eventually finds themselves neck-deep in debt, stuck with a capital investment that went nowhere in a failed attempt to hit one out of the park. However, not accepting defeat, they work on the next break, hoping to strike it rich. There is nothing wrong with that; however, when your economic situation is already in dire straits and chances are more than likely that the condition may worsen, this is no time to roll the dice again.

Previously, failure has happened due to a lack of research, planning, product category, and a lack of knowledge with the flow of goods specific to the industry.

On the other hand, the hobby type of innovator, being hypnotized by the lure of being able to invent and just have bragging rights, will also sometimes find themselves neck-deep in debt because, in a rush to innovate, they overlooked the need to make their product with high quality and at a low cost. As we all know, most of the time there are high costs involved just to be able to accomplish this. However, instead of stopping, the hobby type of innovator continues to pursue his next innovation, and then the next, in a mad attempt to hit the big one that will finally give them the recognition that they are thirsty for. These types of innovators do more harm than good, as they begin to be recognized only as an idea person and not a serious innovator.

Innovators must do their soul-searching before starting to attempt a breakthrough in innovation. Every potential innovator must know whether they are in it for the economics or for the sport. If you find yourself to be in a place to consider an attempt to innovate, it is very important to take a step back and consider this very issue.

The importance of knowing the action plan needed to succeed between these two types of attempted innovators is two worlds apart! This means that if you are in it for the economics, you must be willing to drop everything that you are doing at the time so that you can only work on your innovation and nothing else, period. There is a saying— "whatever it takes"—meaning that if it means traveling, being away from friends and loved ones, and being away from home for long periods of time, you will have to be willing to do it, because in all seriousness, this is what it takes to succeed!

If you are only a tinkerer—or as many of these individuals call themselves, an "idea person"—then don't sweat it; you can afford to just hobby with the notion of one day becoming a serious innovator. However, don't be sad if others don't see you or don't take you seriously when you want to talk about a new idea, for these will be taken as just words in the wind, not to be taken seriously. Keep living your comfortable life, and hopefully one day you won't have regrets about not getting serious!

The Search for Longevity

There are successful innovators who play the long game. This means that they want to see how far their innovations will go in the marketplace. Unfortunately, some of these innovators took so long to reach success that they are now up there in age, and some don't get to see their innovations reach a pinnacle in the marketplace.

It's possible that they did not strive to improve their current lifestyle. We have already mentioned what usually happens when an innovator becomes content and gets lazy. They will not eat better or give themselves time, as they are set in their ways.

However, if you start making a transformation for the better, it is not unlikely to reach longevity for an extra five, 10, 15, or 20-plus years! This is priceless. So if you want to get to see how far your innovation can go in the marketplace, it is time to get started on the road to recovery.

This is not an easy task. It will take getting knowledge about how to make lifestyle changes. This will entail the following:

a. Losing weight, and if overweight, maintaining portion control
b. Improved diet if you are currently overdrinking or overeating sweets, fats, salty foods, beverages, etc.
c. Exercise if you are not currently doing so
d. Alternative therapies, like acupuncture, acupressure, etc.
e. Therapeutic massage
f. Improved personal grooming

g.   Personal improvement counseling

This is a quick list of things that you can do if you are not already that serious about the results of longevity and happiness in your life.

In addition to those benefits, those around you will admire your progress and feel like they should do the same thing. Lead by example, that's what true leaders do!

By doing the above you will be well on your way to seeing your innovation play out to its fullest extent, and you will also be able to profit from it to the max. Who knows—you may still have some more innovations still left inside of you! The payoff potential is too big to pass up. That's why it's imperative that you get started right away on your way to a personal transformation. This effort may take years, especially if it entails diet change or serious weight loss, but don't be disappointed and don't give up. The writer of this book has made most of these changes in his life and has received the benefits of better health, weight loss, and a greater degree of happiness and confidence.

BE A FORCE FOR GOOD

Many companies today focus much effort in progressive social work. A big part of their profits goes back into helping those in need, many times through job training. This is without a doubt an admirable position to be in. This is done in many ways, like selling one item and donating the second one to individuals who need it, and this is a very worthy cause. Other companies give half of their profits to worthy causes, also achieving a very good deed.

You will find out that these companies, regardless of their help for others, can do quite well financially. Their management team is very satisfied and happy, and also very proud that they work for a company that is a "force for good".

A job training program can many times set us apart as a company involved in changing this world by training others with no skills so that they can help themselves. There is a saying: "Feed a man fish and he will eat for one day, show a man how to fish and he will eat for a lifetime".

Yes, you can be a force for good by extending a training work program, especially for those with no skills. The writer recognizes that the costs will add up, but this comes with an advantage of securing a skilled labor force and can be seen as a good, solid investment into the future.

You will also be helping your own community become better off economically by training those with no skills—and you will find out that most of these individuals will become very loyal employees.

The benefit of being a force for good can be very rewarding indeed. You will be recognized by others as a compassionate person and you will be seen as a true leader, as well as a community leader. If this expense of training those with no skills is onerous to you, there may be government benefits for doing it. Many companies move their operations or start their operations in what are called federal- or state-designated enterprise zones. These are areas that are designated as economically disadvantaged zones, so it would be smart to find out if there are such programs in your area. Many tax benefits can be derived from these types of programs, and it is an easy and very low-cost way to start a company.

There will be times when the opportunities that you extend will not be appreciated even by those in need; however, the individuals that will appreciate you and the opportunities that your company offers them will definitely overshadow the individuals who don't appreciate.

ALLIANCES

Many times, making new friends can be difficult, especially in the business setting. However, you will need to do this in order to be well informed about what's going on in the industry. The making of friends will also help you network, and this should help with meeting others in the industry, this is a very important thing to do, especially if you want to continue to grow your business.

The best ways to get to make new friends in the industry is at the tradeshows. The national tradeshows are, many times, the best venues where you can meet company owners or company executives in the industry.

Many times, the best way to get to meet the players in the industry is by simply walking up to them, making a quick personal introduction and telling them what company you're with and what it does. Make sure you have plenty of business cards to pass around. Some of these industry leaders may not warm up to you right away, but it is essential that you meet them and that they are at least made aware of you.

Some of these leaders will quickly respond in a positive way, and may even propose to carry some of your products in their offering. This, of course, is an important decision to make, whether you want to have others involved in the sales of your product or not.

The proper way to be is to always listen closely to any offers and keep an open mind. You never know where your closest ally may come from, or in what form you will be able to further your company growth.

Other effective ways of keeping up with others in the industry is to join what some recognize as buying groups. Meetings are held at least once a year, and they bring together many members in the industry. There are industry groups that also form committees with a special emphasis on what all the industry leaders are doing to grow their businesses. Participation is highly recommended as a valuable networking opportunity. This is also a good way to make new contacts in the industry.

If you are networking with others, you are just increasing your chances of success. So make it a point to always continue and network, making new friends and building valuable alliances that will help your business growth.

TAX REGULATION

As your business grows, there may be challenges that make you question whether you are a true innovator or whether your income is derived from legal activities. These challenges mostly come from government agencies in charge of enforcing laws and making sure that taxes are paid towards workers' accounts for their benefits in case of potential future, work associated injury, retirement, illness, etc.

One of the first focused points of the tax regulators is to question the sources of revenue being reported on your tax form, given the size of a new revenue stream. They may request a meeting and then a follow-up at your home to verify that what you're telling them is true. Once this is confirmed and they are satisfied that your source of revenue is legal, they may move into the next phase of the investigation. This new phase is strictly taxation, in favor of the employees that are now making your new product.

As with all new businesses, you may or may not already have your factory with your own employees. However, it is more than likely that you are not there yet. There may be several reasons for this. It may be that the business has not yet reached that type of growth yet. Or it may be that the innovator does not wish to own their own factory. Whatever the reason, the tax regulators may inquire about such employees. The fact that your business may employ independent contractors may be enough to trigger a taxation audit.

The tax regulators may come with the point of view that, even if it is not your employees making the product, since you are the one that controls the proceeds you will also be made personally responsible for the taxation. This will be something that you do not agree with. You may think, "How is it possible that I become responsible for employees that do not even work for me?" At this point, it will not matter what your point of view may or may not be in regards to this point. The tax regulators will more than likely start an audit and begin the investigation process.

You will more than likely need legal representation, as this issue will likely not be resolved in a few weeks, but rather years. Yes, you may suffer sleepless nights and begin to question whether it would just be easier at this point to start your own production with your own employees. Naturally, this may not be a load that you were looking or even planning to take on; however, given the circumstances and how this seems to be a futile, no-win fight, this may be the time that you start opening your mind to assembling your own production team. We have already considered this topic previously, and the different ways to be able to accomplish it. The smart play would be that once the audit is over, regardless of the outcome, that you and your business are not exposed to a second or even a third bite of the apple by the taxation regulators. You must position your business against these types of traps or dangers all the time and be ever vigilant to these types of attacks.

HIRING PROFESSIONAL HELP

The hiring of professionals to help you guide, mold, and protect your business will be very important as it continues to grow. These professionals will be attorneys with different expertise like business law, patent law, taxation law, etc. There will be a need for a good accountant (or accountants) who will help you primarily with tax issues, tax preparation and possibly, from time to time, auditing triggered by government agencies, insurance companies, or financial institutions that you are trying to borrow money from.

The best way to hire these types of individuals is to get references from them and get to know about them through word of mouth. Many times, you can refer to the Better Business Bureau in your area for information on the businesses, reputation. Once you have decided on what professionals you may be interested in hiring, take the time to interview them, keeping in mind that your businesses' future survival may depend on the decision you are making. Take your time and do a thorough job.

If you do a thorough job and choose the right firms, your company will continue to grow and will continue to thrive moving forward. There is a high value in hiring good, reputable representatives, as their reputation will say much about who you are as a businessperson. This, many times, goes a long way, especially when a need for high integrity is required and when trials get messy; this is when character issues may be used to trump a rival. So always remember that you must do your best to hire the most untouchable individuals, with the best reputations around.

This writer knows a family individual beginning his business. However, this business was going to be partly owned by him, but the majority was to be controlled by a larger corporation. He was excited and was ready to sign the agreement, even though he did not understand the agreement in its entirety. This writer, upon being notified of this, immediately recommended that he start to assemble and hire his professional team immediately. The family individual did not want to go through the motion of hiring legal and tax counsel. He felt that he did not need it. The writer responded that if issues were to arrive later, the individual was not going to have legal recourse, as he had taken it upon himself to sign the agreement without totally understanding it. Fortunately, the family member finally listened and began to seek legal counsel after this.

Never get lazy and try to take shortcuts like this, as it may very well be the issue that brings your downfall.

DOMESTIC VS. INTERNATIONAL SALES

Many new companies begin by creating sales domestically and, once they feel that they have the market share that they desired, move on to seek growing their international sales. This is a hard decision to make for any innovator, for there are many hoops to jump through when it comes to developing international sales. For starters, the requirements to protect your innovation may be complicated and expensive. It will take multiple detailed translations of your innovations' descriptions and require finding legal counsel to represent you in any given country.

You will need to budget three to four times more, as traveling overseas is very expensive and takes much longer. You will need to have your sales materials translated into the different languages where you plan to sell, and you will have to ship samples long distance as well. This will require big budgets before any type of return or pay off can be expected—and some may never pay off.

International sales development takes time and patience, and many times requires hiring employees in the countries you are planning to sell into. This will be a high added cost. Another challenge is the money exchange rate, where many times, due to a strong dollar your innovation will have to be priced higher. This may well discourage any interest in your innovation.

With international sales development you will need to be planning for the long term. The difference in culture can also make things more challenging, and the way goods and services get distributed and sold may be very different than in the U.S. In addition, the business laws may also be different, so you may be better off seeking business counsel in that country, as you will need to secure governmental permission to do business in that country as well. You will need to be aware of many details like these before you make your move and before you attempt entering these different markets. In addition, you may have to depend on a translator if you still do not have an employee in that country.

Yes, the challenges of international sales are big ones and the potential pitfalls are many. But this is another arena where you cannot afford to take shortcuts. You will need much time to plan and have a good strategy in place before going for it. However, if you still have a strong desire to open international markets, then again make sure you do your homework.

International business can be quite lucrative if done right; it also gives the business protection or exposure of being tied to a single market only. The rewards can become quite considerable.

GAUGING THE FUTURE

All the planning and strategizing in the world cannot predict the future; however, you can plan to have contingencies in place in case your industry is swept by winds of change, which can affect your business beyond your control. Another thing that can be hard to predict are economic recessions. These may be short- or long-lived. It will be important going forward that you have liquid assets that you can use to bridge your business to survive them. If you do, your company will come out of the situation stronger than ever. However, to get to this point, you must plan for these economic downturns. It's not situations of *if* they will happen, but *when*. These downturns are just a part of a changing global market. So, plan accordingly.

If your industry is in change or turmoil despite a good economy, this is a whole different situation that may have to be addressed differently. Industry changes can come in different forms, such as government regulation changes, code regulation changes, standard changes, etc. They may end up being beyond your control, and you may find yourself on the losing side of change. In this case, there will be no other alternative but to try to innovate out of this situation—or, if that is not economically possible at the time, you may have to consider selling the business, or closing the business down and walking away with as many assets as possible before all is lost.

The actual personal age of the innovator is an important consideration, as well as their health, which can foretell the future of the company or its leadership. In this case, gauging the future becomes much easier to predict. On the bright side, these are circumstances that can be predicted and can allow the innovator the time to plan the best road to proceed. Much thought should be given as to how long the innovator can keep going and how effectively they can continue to run the business. Ones the decision has been made as to the passing of the torch, steps need to be taken that are well-planned and organized, so as not to affect the organization negatively while these changes take place.

The changes may be a transition of leadership in some situations; in those cases, the change can be much smoother, as pretty much everything stays the same and only the leadership changes. In cases of a change in ownership, many changes can happen, as the new ownership will be looking into all options so its new investment will run as efficiently as possible. This often requires moving the company to another region of the country. It is also more than likely that consolidation will take place. This will shrink the number of employees and require positions to be moved to the new location. This may or may not be an option offered to existing employees.

Yes, the future may be hard to gauge; however, never stop planning for it, as the winds of change will surely come. Make sure you are well prepared when they do.

THERE IS NO TOMORROW

When planning to innovate, there is no time to waste. Some windows of innovation may be more time restrained than others. In an industry that moves fast, all innovators need to keep this in mind. One of the most disheartening things that can happen in innovation is to have your inventions rejected by the patent office because another innovator beat you to the punch. Always keep in mind that if you are thinking about an innovation, others are thinking of it as well.

It is not uncommon to get told by others in the industry, while you are introducing your product, that they thought of the same idea before you ever did, but never did anything about it. Individuals that did not do anything about their idea are likely saddened with regret when they see another person introducing an innovation that they had previously thought about.

There could be many different reasons for this. Most would-be innovators procrastinate, some just don't have the proceeds to innovate, and others may not have the confidence in their idea—therefore, they forfeit to others what may represent millions of dollars towards their economic futures.

If a would-be innovator is stuck in a bad economic situation, but could experience being in the million-dollar club of innovation success for at least a day, chances are that they would never even think of procrastinating. The fact that an innovation could set them up for economic security for the rest of their lives is reason enough to do whatever it takes to come out with their innovation, no matter the hurdles or cost.

So, the next time that you think of passing up on an innovation opportunity, remember that even though there are no guarantees of success, you may very well be sitting on a winner. Many times, the difference between success and failure lies squarely on the innovator's shoulders, as decisions and strategy can make all the difference as to whether the innovation will be a success or a failure. Therefore, planning must be done without shortcuts, and strategy should be well defined before starting any innovation work.

Again, keep in mind of the old saying that "time is money." It is not easy to innovate fast, when much planning needs to be done; however, this balance must go hand in hand. Innovation success is many times won by being the fastest to market in combination with also being the most efficient.

Grooming Your Organization

The practice of keeping a neat and tidy appearance is very important for any organization. The organizations with tidy operations and well-groomed personnel gain respect in the industry. Much of a company's success depends on the appearance that it gives off to its customers and potential customers. The more well-groomed a company appears to be, the greater the amount of success it will have.

You, as an employer, can introduce a dress code if you don't have one, and can begin to enforce it, as well. Not only can the clothes that an employee wears be regulated, but also things like hair, piercings, tattoos, nails, etc.

The company's headquarters also needs to give off a professional and clean look. This is not an easy-to-accomplish feat, so it may be easier to hire personnel or an independent contractor to focus and take care of it.

A maintenance contractor may be somebody that you may want to hire if your building is aged and is in need of repairs. The landscape area is another space that is very important to keep well-trimmed and groomed, especially given that most of the time this space is exposed to the public.

It is impossible for any company to be successful for the long term if it does not have a professional appearance. No company will continue to grow unless it takes care of its appearance. A company that is well-groomed is not only more professional looking but is also much more efficient. This can easily be lost if the company is not constantly being run well groomed.

Cleanliness is a lifestyle; however, and unfortunately, not all humans are the same when it comes to cleanliness. The more you practice, the more benefits will come to you and your business. By setting a high standard of cleanliness within your company, your employees will be able to work in a more comfortable environment. This adds value to your company and its employees.

Always remember that the way to plan and strategize for long term success is to set a high standard of grooming company and then constantly enforce it.

Day-to-Day Operations

Day-to-day operations do not have to be hard work for an innovator. Every day does not have to become a grind.

Any innovator who is experiencing company growth can start feeling overwhelmed, especially if the growth is explosive. It is in these cases that the innovator must begin thinking of running a company and building an organization. This sounds easier than it really is.

To build an organization it takes time, energy, patience, and money. However, if you feel that this is the only way to continue, and growth continues to appear to be inevitable, this step must be taken.

A tactic that may help an innovator begin to build an organization as the company grows is by hiring some key management positions, then allowing these individuals to interview and choose which applicants will be hired. It is important to note that every new hire will require much paperwork, and this will take a person experienced in human resources.

Eventually, things will stabilize, the team will be hired, and training must follow. This must include discussing the strategy that the company will use in order to be able to grow and succeed, in spite of heavy competition down the road. Each individual who is being hired must be able to engrave the business strategy in their heads—especially management positions and all positions in sales and marketing.

The strategy must cover details regarding present sales, future sales targets, present market share information, market penetration projections, target lists of potential customers, etc. However, the most important discussion is the method that will be used to reach the future desired results. This can come in a form of sales promotions, marketing drives, targeted sales drives, purchasing terms being extended, etc.

The strategy must also include a detailed training period for all sales personnel to make sure that the message going forward is clear, concise, and most importantly convincing enough to develop into future sales.

The sales training program may need to include the videotaping of each salesperson as they deliver their message. This will allow them to view their own progress going forward. There must be a training panel that will grade the sales personnel on their oration, level of confidence, body language, grooming, facial expressions, clarity, etc.

PROJECTIONS

Before any innovator commits to a project, it is of the upmost importance to see the best chances of success.

In order to do this, you will have to have a good idea about the numerous issues going forward. For example, the size of the space within the marketplace, the perceived value of the space, the price that the market will bear for your innovation, the projected units to be sold per year, the amount of competition, the penetration potential, and your real sales potential versus the competitions offering.

This would be the solution:

100,000 total market – 20,000 = 80,000 total potential units that may apply x $150 = $12,000,000 total projected sales potential within industry – 80% realistic penetration potential = $9,600,000

The total revised amount must then be divided by the competitors to include yourself:

3 total competitors – 33% market share each = $3,168.000 units per year

If your innovation will take a considerable amount of investment—and this will overshadow the expected return on investment—then it would be a good idea to put the innovation on hold and not resume until a lower cost can be achieved, or until any updated projected information would seriously move the needle upward.

The above-illustrated calculations are only a quick demonstration of a calculated projection, and this writer recommends a much more detailed and in depth calculation being taken from industry numbers based on reliable sources.

This must be done by professional with business education. If you don't have such a person as part of your organization, be sure to hire an independent contractor that specializes in this kind of work. It may be well worth it.

If you find that the planned innovation does not fit your financial criteria, there still may be a way to salvage it. Also, there still may be potential in capitalizing on your idea. This would mean that instead of developing your innovation and marketing it in the industry, you would work to secure a patent and then sell the idea with the patent rights. There may be others in the industry who might want to develop and offer products within your idea's space.

WEATHER CATASTROPHIES

With increased occurrences of extreme weather, chances are that all of us will be affected by it in one way or another. Whether you believe in climate change or not is beside the point.

The fact that all industries will feel the sting of changing weather is a fact. Just looking at the news, it is not difficult to find small island countries being submerged back into the ocean and huge metropolitan countries, like Indonesia, where its capital, Jakarta, is having to move because it is sinking and being overtaken by the ocean.

From tornadoes, hurricanes, earthquakes, mudslides, fires, tsunamis, typhoons, etc. depending in what region of the world we find ourselves, we will never be immune from having to face extreme weather conditions. The other difficult thing that this can affect in a negative way—besides being a danger to our families and us personally—is also to our businesses.

Economics are really at stake due to extreme weather. Every innovator needs to access their exposure to this situation and consult their insurance experts about having enough coverage should a weather occurrence ever affect their business. Extreme weather events can pose great dangers, from ruined factories to damaged inventory and delays in deliveries to broken supply lines.

So make sure to not become a victim of an extreme weather occurrence and make sure that your business is properly insured and covered. If confronted by something like this, you'll be glad that you are. It's not a matter of *if* it happens but more like *when* it will happen.

Technology

Many times, a business can rush into adopting a new technology, whether it's a new computer, new software, a new machine, new automation method, new robotics, etc.

However, rushing into new technology may be a big mistake, as some of the new technology may not be ready to be used in a business setting, and the investment might not make any sense. New technology can be very expensive, and before being purchased, it must be able to pay its own way.

As with many things that a business can purchase, it can turn out to be overkill. Overkill in the business world oftentimes refers to the fact that a business is not at the point where it can use the new technology—which is the opposite of a new technology that is not ready to be used in a business setting yet.

Technology needs to be assessed carefully before being adopted. Remember that the goal is that by introducing it, it must help the business grow and to help either gain sales, increase production, save time processing, etc.

It is possible that forcing technology upon a growing business can become a distraction and a disruptor. Now, disruption is not necessarily a bad thing. However, if the new technology is not a good fit for the business, it would be better not to try and adopt it.

The high cost of human resources is also an important thing to factor in before adopting new technology. The technology may make it necessary to train your employees on it, and this may take countless hours that the business cannot afford.

The high cost of new technology can also leave a business so in debt that even using the new technology can end up being so expensive that it does not merit the investment. It can leave a business so in debt that it can become paralyzed and few options are left for it to invest for additional growth in sales, marketing or any other areas until the debt is paid off. New technology can create a big toll of missed opportunities if the business is not ready for it.

On the other side of the coin, new technology—when brought in at the right time of the business cycle and mastered at the same time—can bring an unprecedented explosion of added efficiencies and profits to any business.

Achievement

Any innovator that has brought to market a numerous amount of new innovations and succeeded has accomplished a great feat that few have been able to reach. This achievement will follow them with a lifetime of recognition and admiration from others.

Most innovators go deep into their memory well of knowledge, which may include past experiences like the hard knocks of life, failures, losses, the agony of defeat, belittling from others, fear, etc., just to get to where they are now. These are places and situations where most human beings would not even dare expose themselves to.

Achievement means "a thing done successfully typically by effort, courage, or skill."

One of the best synonym words for achievement is "winning."

Innovators must always be careful not to allow themselves to gamble with their fates. Fate means "the development of events beyond a person's control, regarded as determined by a supernatural power."

One of the best synonym words for fate is "providence."

Innovators must always remember that they are not innovators by providence or because they are the chosen ones. Innovating is a personal choice!

History is littered with the ruin of many human beings including countries that believed that it was their providence to win countless battles and some even to conquer the entire world.

Many innovators can expose themselves to failure by trying to do the same thing repeatedly hoping to end up with a different result; however, this turns into madness. As an innovator, you must always do your research and stalk the odds in your favor. Never think that you will break out with a grand slam because it's providence or just because it's your destiny. Leaving things up to chance may become an innovator's ruin, as history shows.

Once you have done your research, gather all your winning thoughts and methods and continue to get the odds stacked in your favor just like you have done in the past. By always using this strategy, it is more than likely that you will continue to win!

SELF-ESTEEM

Attempting to innovate is a difficult thing to do. Becoming a successful innovator is almost always impossible to accomplish. Innovators who succeed almost always become multi-millionaires.

This becomes a lifestyle, as the successful innovator climbs into an economic upswing like they have never experienced before. It is during this climb that a successful innovator will start to experience self-esteem. Many innovators who are still on their journeys to success do not have self-esteem because of the many uncertain situations that they are faced with. So instead, they suffer from low self-esteem.

Low self-esteem is difficult to get rid of; it is a lack of confidence and feeling badly about oneself. Innovators with low self-esteem often feel unloved, awkward, or incompetent.

If an innovator suffers from low self-esteem, their chances of succeeding are almost none. In order to become a successful innovator, low self-esteem must be conquered. Many times, we have been told that we are no good, that our ideas will never work, that we will never amount to anything, or that we will never become successful. This programming, if not shaken, can get ahold of us and we will start to believe the lie. As soon as we believe the lie, it becomes self-fulfilling and we will begin to act accordingly.

This is one of the dangers for innovators, as this type of work requires confidence and self-esteem. If you are surrounded by negative people, you must get out of those types of friendships or even relationships, as negative people will always try to bring you down. Always remember that misery loves company.

So as you move into your lifelong journey to success, one of the most important things that you must consistently do is to weed out the people who are negative and that one way or another will help you bring feelings of doubt and low self-esteem into your abilities.

ETHICS

As you venture off on your journey to success, you will need to always be ethical regarding decisions or actions that you or your company will practice. Ethics are very important in business and especially in life. Without a high standard of ethics, it will become quite difficult to become successful in the long term. There is a wise saying: "You reap what you sow."

Naturally if we sow lemons, we can never expect to reap oranges. The same is true in business and in life. We can only expect what we have planted, nothing more and nothing less. Having a high standard of ethics is not only good for business but will always be something that will make you feel good about yourself and will guarantee you a great personal reputation.

Again, having and practicing a high standard of ethics is good for business, as this will also make others want to join your organization because of the good reputation recognition that you have earned.

The word ethics is defined as "moral principles that govern a person's behavior or the conducting of an activity."

Some good synonyms for the word ethics are the following: moral principles, rules of conduct, and standards of behavior.

So important was good conduct in displaying ethics that famous philosophers such as Plato, Aristotle, and Socrates wrote about the subject.

Plato wrote that ethics brings wisdom, temperance, courage, and justice.

Socrates wrote that ethics brings courage, self-control, and justice.

Aristotle wrote that ethics brings good, righteousness, and happiness.

Yes, these were wise men and many of their teachings are still thought in our top universities around the world.

The Greeks practiced the word "ethos". It means "character" and is used to describe the guiding beliefs or ideals that characterize a community, nation, or ideology.

The Greeks were able to accomplish great feats as a nation, conquering many others and eventually becoming a world power. By practicing ethos, or ethics, they accomplished a meeting of the minds with their citizens, and therefore became a very strong country—the first country to ever practice democracy.

VISION

As you navigate through your journey to success, you will find out that creating a successful innovation and company will require vision. Vision is very important to have, as it will help you as a guide on key decisions that only you will be able to make. Your fundamental success will depend first and foremost on your vision. Without vision, you will be lost in the woods, not knowing what direction to take on your journey to success.

The word vision is defined as "a thought, concept, or object formed by the imagination."

Using vision also includes imagination, and the definition for imagination is "the faculty or action of forming new ideas, or images or concepts of external objects, not present to the senses."

Of course, without the use of imagination, an innovator will never become successful with their ideas, as they will lack imagination or creativity.

Without vision, what the innovator plans to do will more than likely fail, as they will lack the proper creativity that is required to hit a grand slam. When we refer to a grand slam, we are talking about something that will introduce an innovator into a tier of wealth they have never experienced before. This will also come along with recognition in the industry.

The abovementioned grand slam innovation, when successful, will generate so much revenue that it will introduce the innovator into a high standard of living facilitated by repeat business that will be generated for the rest of their life. We are not talking about a limited form of success—we are talking about a titanic shift in the lifestyle of the innovator and their family. This type of breakthrough innovation will bring legacy status to the innovator, should they hit the proverbial grand slam.

Hitting the grand slam requires planning, technique, vision, endurance, and courage. There are only a few athletes who have ever accomplished grand slams, especially when the setting is the World Series. So, when the lights and the pressure are on you, and the pressure to be bold is being applied, you will need all these virtues to accomplish a feat that only a few have been able to.

Never forget that in using vision, and continue to envision the impossible, you will discover that once you train your mind to think this way, it will make problem-solving simple and the impossible will become very possible to accomplish.

COMMON SENSE

Some actions that are made, or decisions that are expected to be made, especially by employees or others, many times are not made in the right way. However, there is no way to predict how others will take action or make decisions. Even though some call it "using common sense," in this more complex world, there is no such thing!

As an innovator, never expect others to use what you would view as common sense. The fact is, if you continue to think that others will use what you view as a common-sense approach, you will likely be constantly disappointed.

Employees are many times the ones who will disappoint an innovator, especially when an innovator is expected to find that the decision or action taken was not made in the manner that they expected.

This writer's father, who was a businessperson for many years, always used the expression, "It's just common sense!" At the time, the writer agreed, especially hearing directly from his father about the many mistakes that were being made in his business because of the lack of so-called "common sense."

The father had many employees and for years always complained about their lack of common sense. Unfortunately, years later he died, frustrated and broke, in many ways due to the lack of common sense that his employees lacked.

After witnessing his father's downfall, this writer began to change his view about how the word "common sense" is applied in the business setting. He came to the conclusion that in order to fix this from occurring constantly, all innovators must make sure to never expect common sense from others. The writer decided to set his ideology about this in a different way, thinking and then believing that common sense is not so common after all!

After changing his ideology, this writer began to never think or expect that others would use common sense—especially in the way that he expected. The writer began using this same approach, learning from his father's mistakes, and changed from using a common-sense approach to using a "meeting of the minds approach."

This can only be accomplished by planning and making sure that all the plans are documented for the team to review, memorize, understand and then put into practice. This takes patience to be allowed to develop using very detailed and precise communication. If done in this manner, the results will speak for themselves.

PARANOIA

Many businesspeople say that you need a certain measure of paranoia to become successful. To a certain extent this may be true. The fact that there is a phrase that goes "you must never rest on your laurels" is proof of this. This phrase has been used for many centuries, from the times that the Greek athletes were awarded laurels as the top prize for winning in athletic competition.

The meaning of the phrase "not to rest on your laurels" means to not relax or not to get lazy just thinking about past wins; instead, the need is to keep looking forward to other wins. The successful innovator never relaxes, but instead is always looking for the next innovation or to keep expanding sales and markets for their current one. This takes a certain amount of constant motion and energy. Traveling also becomes a necessity as the business expands.

The constant worry about competition is also cause for having to move fast always making sure of not getting lazy. This is may be a big problem in organizations that reach a certain size, and it could easily be thought that sales will always be there. The problem with this thought process is that innovation changes quickly and that the competition also wants to grow and stymie any company that it perceives as being a danger to its future.

Therefore, sales teams must always stay motivated to keep growing the business. Again, as we discussed in past chapters, it's a jungle out there. The jungles are full of cannibals who want to eat you for breakfast and leave your carcass out for wild animals to feed on. The hyenas will move in to complete the job. The competition not only wants to eat your lunch; it is hunting you down to kill you so that you stop competing with them.

You need to stay vigilant and on course using your original plan and agreed-upon path. Not doing so can bring serious consequences, as this can become your downfall—and eventually your doom.

Paranoia has something to do with not being able to relax or sleep, and this may be a good thing to have, as it can keep you vigilant and on your toes all the time. In the business world, this is important to safeguard so you notice oncoming dangers.

So, coming from the specific application for the business world, the word "paranoia" must not be used in the medical way, as in the condition of mental illness. Paranoia in the medical industry is recognized as a mental condition characterized by delusions of persecution, unwarranted jealousy, or exaggerated self-importance, typically elaborated into an organized system. The innovator must never apply the medical definition to their business.

Sixth Sense

There does exist an inner voice in some of us human beings that warns us to the unknown, many times about dangers that may be heading our way.

This inner voice is something that each innovator must always be aware of and make sure not to ignore. It is what many call a "sixth sense." It is also commonly referred to as "following your gut feeling".

The ability is not possessed by everyone or used by all, and all innovators would be smart to acquire this valuable ability.

When running a business, success or failure can depend on whether or not we listen to our sixth sense. When innovating an innovator many times has the difficult job of deciding which way to go with their ideas or what the market will prefer as to features and benefits on their innovation. At these moments is when the sixth sense can help.

If you do not posses this valuable tool as an innovator you must make a concerted effort to acquire it. By paying attention to ideas, insights, and impressions that seem to come out of nowhere, you can develop your own intuitive sixth sense.

Again, this can make all the difference between success or failure. Most of the time, innovators do not have the room to make mistakes or adjustments. Only the big companies have that luxury.

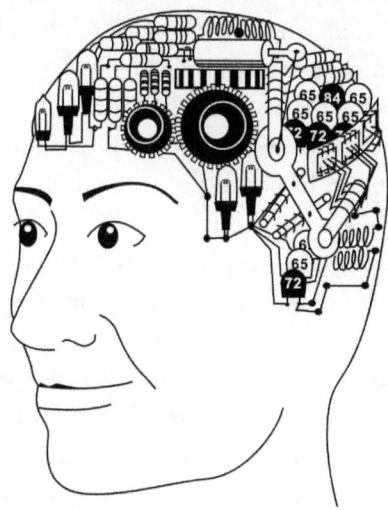

IMAGINATION

Some individuals have tapped into their imaginations and this has created great wealth for them. Some examples are Walt Disney, Steve Jobs, and Jeff Bezos, to name a few.

To become a successful innovator, you must harness the power of imagination, especially when it comes to innovation. This is where the innovators excel, as many times they have the imagination to see a future idea that has the potential of creating great wealth. Again, good examples of these are the Disneyland Amusement Parks, the iPhone cell phone, and the Amazon online shopping site.

All, of the abovementioned innovators used their imagination to innovate, then proceeded to create vehicles that only they could imagine at the time, and that changed the world. These innovations created fortunes for them, and still continue to produce great wealth to this day.

It is not easy to reach that level of success. In simpler terms, it is damn hard! However, even then, would you not also like to be able to reach these levels of success, during your lifetime?

Nothing is impossible to accomplish!

Rest assured that even the abovementioned innovators were told by others to stop dreaming and that their ideas would never become a reality. However, they never gave up until they accomplished the very thing their imaginations led them to, proving that imagination has much to do with being a successful innovator, as it is the foundation of truly great ideas. A great idea always starts with using the imagination before it can materialize and become a reality.

The power of using our God-given brain allows us to imagine things that still don't exist but that may be possible to accomplish. It is easy to just come up with ideas; pretty much anyone can do that. However, the power of using our imaginations can change the world if the imagination is thinking of a grandiose idea, and the idea is followed up with dedication until it materializes into a product or service.

Imagination by itself will never be enough to make you a great innovator; remember it is just the foundation of all great ideas. It will also take dedication, passion, patience, energy, resources, planning, among other things to create that great success that all innovators are chasing, yes, the proverbial grand slam.

PREVENTION

We have all heard the saying "an ounce of prevention is worth a pound of cure." This means that precautions must be taken before making key decisions, as the costs or losses could be quite heavy if prevention is not used. A simple example of this is when the engine oil light in your automobile kicks on and warns you that the oil needs to be changed, but you don't make time to take it into the service department to get changed because you're just too busy! Well, let's now think what a "little prevention" could have saved you from if you would have only just taken your vehicle to have the oil changed when the light came on.

First your engine goes out in the middle of the road as you were on your way to a meeting where you were to pitch a very motivated group of investors that was excited about your innovation. So, you now have to cancel the meeting.

Second, since you are in the middle of the road stranded, now you have to call a towing company to have your vehicle towed to the mechanic.

Third, you now have to rent a vehicle so that you have transportation while your vehicle's engine gets repaired or replaced.

You have now suddenly lost a day of production, compared to maybe losing an hour in taking your vehicle to the mechanic. And worst of all is that you just got a call from your mechanic with the very bad news that your engine needs to be replaced and will cost you $5,000. It is now when you suddenly regret "not using prevention" by taking your vehicle to the mechanic. In comparison, it would have only cost $49.95 to get your oil changed. That is what many call the proverbial "ounce of prevention."

But this is not the only pain that you may go through. Now, because you did not heed your oil light warning, you have to tell your family that the yearly planned family vacation will need to be canceled because you ignored your vehicle light. And so the money that was earmarked for the vacation must now be used to pay the mechanic. You can imagine what will happen next: your spouse will be very upset, your kids may start crying, and the family dog, sensing that you messed up, won't even want to get close to you.

This example shows how using prevention can prevent having to lose time, energy, face, and wasted resources that many times we just don't have at the moment.

Therefore, when applied to business, you must always use prevention. By doing so, you will avoid many headaches and heartaches. All successful innovators use prevention, and with time they begin to accumulate great wealth because of its application and enforcement.

FORESIGHT

Foresight has much to do with being a leader.

There is no doubt that those individuals that possess foresight are seasoned veterans who can for see the future. This does not come automatically; instead, it comes with years of experience and knowing what works in business or your industry and what does not work.

A good leader will always lead their team away from danger and will do everything within their power to protect the team as much as they can.

Again, we are talking about all of this while you are on your journey to success with all the dangers that lurk out there. These are dense jungles full of cannibals and wild animals that are looking for their next meal. These predators will not have any mercy on you and will finish you off with any chance you give them. They are bloodthirsty and, even if not hungry, some kill for the sheer sport of it. They then leave the carcasses of their kill for other predators to finish off.

Again, don't fool yourself: it's a jungle out there, with countless dangers lurking around every corner. Therefore, good leaders will always plan and work on having a contingency plan so that their team has alternatives for a quick escape if need be.

Now you may be asking yourself, why is this writer again going back to how nasty and dangerous it is out there? So, the simple reason is that an innovator should never expect any different in a free market society like the one that we do business in it is the smartest, boldest, shrewdest, and the one with the best idea that wins success over the long term. Even if you have not yet been confronted with these predators eventually be assured that you will, the competition is always out there observing you and stocking you for an opportunity to take your business away. Just like hungry animals, if you become successful, they will sniff you out and will begin to hunt you down.

Foresight will give you a gut feeling when you are in the most danger of being attacked. You must prepare for those moments in a way where you can attack or strike back. These preparations may include contingency plans like bringing out the next round of innovations, price discounting, extended payment terms, added services, quicker shipping, etc.

Of course, you should never give away something that you don't need to unless it is important enough to keep the business or to block others from gaining access to your customer base.

Again, foresight will tell you when, where, and in what way to keep your business protected at any given time.

FRUSTRATION

There will be many times when an innovator feels frustrated in business. This could be because the idea is not been received well in the industry, pricing seems to be more than what the market is willing to bear, competition all of a sudden is taking customers, employees are not motivated, financing is becoming next to impossible to secure, the company is losing money, etc.

There are a whole host of issues that can become frustrating to the innovator, especially when they are starting out. Frustration will be a constant companion in the beginning—and to a certain point, that is normal. However, as the organization grows, this should be of concern.

As the organization grows, the innovator must set forward a team that will help them run the day-to-day operation and training. This needs to be a fundamental goal for the organization. It is important that frustration always remain in check.

The definition of the word frustration is "the feeling of being upset or annoyed, especially because of inability to change or achieve something."

No one likes working for a mad dog that is always upset or annoyed. So, innovators need to be aware of this and make sure that they stay cool under pressure—even when they are internally frustrated.

The building of an experienced team is of the utmost importance when growing a business. This will prevent frustration and will help you to concentrate on other aspects of the business, like growing it, protecting it, coming up with the next innovation, securing financing, etc.

The innovator only needs to be involved in creating the positive building blocks of the company while his team takes care of the day to day frustrations of on ongoing growing operation.

This may also have the healing effect of keeping negative health conditions, like stress, hyper- tension, high blood pressure, in check.

Again, innovators must always shield themselves from becoming frustrated as this can become very destructive if not kept under control. So if you begin to feel frustrated, take the time to calm down by using a time out: maybe a few days off to take your mind off the business would be appropriate, or going and playing a round of golf, or anything that you can enjoy.

MUTINY

We discussed the destructive power of being frustrated and the reasons that can cause frustration to happen.

We also discussed how no one likes to work for a mad dog, or a boss who is angry or annoyed all the time. So, we are touching on the possible effects that frustration can start. The first word that comes to mind is mutiny.

After anger sets in within an organization, it may take a while to rear its ugly head while it metastasizes. Whether this takes a few days or years, once it does it will explode to the point of no return—like cancer cells inside the body sitting painlessly and waiting for the opportunity to explode. When they do, that's when death becomes possible. This may take a while. As in the human body, first the cells begin to infect other cells, and once they get strong, they begin to affect the human body in a negative way. Eventually the human body will become weakened and find itself so ill that it will lose its mobility and eventually die.

Just like the human body can die due to cancer cells spreading inside, so can any organization that has employees. Each can begin to get infected by the form of frustration that the innovator is displaying. They will begin to feel that the business is out of control and that it lacks good leadership. Eventually they will stop obeying direct orders and disarray will follow, and the business will be forced to close its doors and die.

This is a death that did not have to happen. If the innovator developed a team to run the day-to-day operations, they would not have needed to show frustration to their employees. Instead, that started a string of events that once it grew, could not be stopped—just like a runaway fire that burns out of control.

Can you imagine being a ship captain out in the middle of the ocean and suddenly, the crew will not obey your commands, starts to rebel and moves to take the authority away from you? This would surely be a calamity. Distant in the past as this sounds, it happens with real companies in all the time.

So again, the innovator must do everything in their power to not get involved with the day to day operation unless it is an emergency, short of this, stay away from it and employ your time in innovation and growing the business.

REVENGE

When an innovator shows frustration, they may truly affect their employees' performance, and this may also affect their mental health. This may be called mental cruelty—especially when frustration is accompanied with the use of profanity, acts of punishment, or bullying.

This can be accompanied by resentment and eventually with feelings of wanting to get even with the boss—or sometimes with the whole company. It can be very dangerous, as some individuals may be mentally affected to the point where they will begin to take steps to bring bodily harm to the innovator or to others in the company.

What may be possible is that this mentally unbalanced individual will begin to amass weapons that have the ability to cause damage at great human toll.

Unfortunately, this happens almost daily in this country, with no end in sight. Innocent people may lose their lives for the simple reason that frustration was allowed, to exist and thrive in the company.

Can you imagine one day coming to work and suddenly finding yourself facing an ex-employee armed with an AK 47 assault rifle and having the look of a bloodthirsty madman looking to shoot anyone in his path? Now what would make this even scarier is that you are inside your office working and minding your own business, and suddenly you get trapped by this demon. What do you do? Do you charge this person? Do you yell and scream for help? No doubt that this is the stuff of nightmares! More than likely you would be shot either way, and only by the grace of God would you survive.

The main question is, is it all worth it going through all of this just for a quick display of frustration at the company—then letting it get out of control? Certainly not! Therefore, you can see how this could affect your business in a very bad way.

There is another possibility, and this one has to do with legalities. When employees feel like they have been wronged or mistreated, some of them are willing to start legal proceedings against the company they work for. They will seek out legal counsel who will listen to their complains, and if the counsel feels that there is a case, they could sue the company. The lawsuit may result in a settlement or a court judgement if it goes that far. Either way, this is sometimes a significant amount of money and does not include the attorney fees that will also have to be paid.

Revenge has a way to cause severe and, many times, permanent damage to all those who are affected by it. So, all innovators would be smart to heed this advice and protect themselves from these potential dangers.

BALANCE

One of the ultimate traits in business is to be able to have personal balance—and to be able to build a business with good balance. Balance is defined as "keeping or putting something in a steady position so that it does not fall."

When you are building your business, as your innovation prospers, you should be eager to build a business that has good balance so that it will not topple when under pressure.

Just as you would construct a building, the need for the structure to be kept erect, or true, will be important as you build upward. This will ensure that as you build upward, the building will end up being straight and balanced. The last thing that you need is for your building to lean, as this will cause limitations on how far up you can build before the whole thing topples. The result is if it is built straight, the building will not fall due to having good balance.

In turn, the same goes for building a business. You will have to be patient, take your time and create balance, making sure that every department has a symbiotic relationship with each other. This will take time, but it will ensure that your business will be strong and balanced, and that it won't easily get toppled.

However, now that we have covered how important balance is in business, it's equally important to build or develop balance with yourself personally. But why? For the simple reason that without this, businesses get affected negatively if the leader is not well balanced. We have already covered some scenarios of how this would be possible.

Personal balance covers living by a code, or an ethos. We have already covered the importance of how important it is to live and to do business using a high standard. This means using a high sense of morality, honesty, good judgement, and overall living by the golden rule. If you fall in your personal life due to a lack of balance, for sure your business will be next. This, many times begins to appear as divorce, partner breakups, family disagreements, lawsuits, employee rebellions and other things.

We cannot tell each other how to live our lives, but if we want to build a long and sustainable business—and at the same time, live a long and happy life full of successes—make sure that everything you do is with good balance.

Always remember that practicing the "golden rule" can serve as a constant reminder to consistently practice good balance in everything that you do. If you do, you won't be sorry that you did, as countless dividends will continue to come your way!

SKEPTICISM

We have already discussed the many traits and qualities that can lead us to success in business and in our personal lives.

However, skepticism is one of the qualities that can get in the way of success if not kept in check. Naturally, skepticism could be an important trait to have when others are proposing a business deal. Many things can go wrong, so using caution and skepticism could be a good thing.

When innovating, having skepticism can be more of a negative trait. One of the descriptions of skepticism is "the theory that certain knowledge is impossible."

Now, if all innovators were to use skepticism when innovating, none of them would succeed, for they would start thinking the moment that the first road block hits them, "Oh, this is too hard and it is impossible to resolve the challenge because it is impossible to have the knowledge to keep going further, so I give up!"

Contrary to the skeptical argument is the fact that when innovators begin to innovate, not all the answers are at their disposal. The reason for this is that, in theory, most individuals have no knowledge of something that still does not exist. Even for the innovator, most or much of the knowledge is not available and will have to be gained, acquired, or learned, before they can move forward.

For some humans, skepticism is a natural human trait; they cannot entirely get rid of it and no doubt this is part of a defense mechanism that was infused for personal survival. Additionally, some humans naturally seem to be able to show more skepticism than others.

Again, this writer is not saying that skepticism is a bad trait to have; just that, especially for innovators, skepticism must be kept in check or else this will become a barrier that will make success impossible to achieve.

When building a business, skepticism can be a good thing as to prevent from making quick or bad choices. It should take a certain amount of skepticism. As the company grows and potential employees are being interviewed, the hiring managers should do everything in their power to ensure that the applicant is providing accurate information about themselves. This will ensure that the positions are given to the appropriate people. This is the one place where using skepticism in overabundance is a good thing, as these individuals are still strangers to you, and you don't know whether they are who they say they are. In addition, following up on the information provided by the applicant will ensure that you will make the best decision possible.

REFLECTION

We can all agree that we all live in a modern, busy and complex environment these days. We are all running to our next appointment and we are constantly juggling our daily schedules, our careers and our personal lives. This oftentimes does not allow us to stay focused and can be very distracting. The new trait for us to be able to keep up is multitasking.

However, taking and finding the time to reflect is very important as you innovate and as your company grows. It is impossible to not reflect professionally and stay on top of what is needed to help your innovation reach the next level.

If you have a business to run, reflection needs to be exercised in order to stay on top of the day to day operations, product inventories, employee schedules, deliveries, customer shipping requirements, etc.

Reflection also helps the innovator foresee future needs that will be required for the business, leaving the necessary time to secure what is needed and continue to move forward.

The worst way to run a business is to always be playing defense, for it is harder to score defensively than be able to formulate a plan to score offensively. Reflection also allows the opportunity to communicate with fellow employees about what is new and what is needed to continue to have success in the future.

The need for a leader to plan the strategy for the company is very important moving forward. This is what is called "having a plan." Reflecting on ideas that will help formulate a detailed plan, for the future is important for a leader, as this process will allow the ideas to remain well established.

The "meeting of the minds" process with your business team is also important. It will also take reflection to plan and communicate with them. Unless some time is spent on or invested in reflection this will not be possible. Your leadership role will be limited if you don't give yourself time to reflect. Reflection is part of the process required to succeed. In a fast-changing business environment, you cannot take the chance to *not* reflect on the overall picture of your business. You may become out of touch with what is going on with your organization and with what the present and future will be to ensure the growth that you are looking for.

Do yourself a favor and take some of the time off your busy schedule to always reflect on your organization. The time invested will be well worth it.

DENIAL

Sometimes the truth is hard to accept, especially in business, when the information shows us that things are not going well. It is during these times that many innovators, instead of facing reality and accepting the facts, instead go into a denial phase.

Denial is much easier to assert for by using it things don't have to be changed. It is not uncommon to see innovators who now have mature and established businesses being quite comfortable, and it's easy to think that, for them, that if things are working, why change them? This, to certain point is fine; however, the words "if things are working" are the catch.

When things are not working, the following happens: sales are down, profits are down, employee morale is down, vendors are unhappy because of slow or no pay, customers are leaving because delivery of your goods or services takes too long, etc.

These are the times when the reality is cashflow is down because there is not enough profit, and there is not enough profit because there are not enough sales, and there is slow payment of vendors because your company's delivery process is taking too long, therefore affecting your receivables in a very negative way. Employee morale is down because they see what is going on, and yet the innovator will not accept that things have to be changed and refuses to accept the situation and is full of denial.

Once conditions like those are allowed, it is very difficult to reverse them. Sometimes the only other alternative may be bankruptcy reorganization, however there is no assurance that the court will agree to this. If it were to be attempted, it would not be uncommon to end up in a bankruptcy liquidation instead of a reorganization. This all depends if the court feels that the business is not too far gone and that it is in the creditors' best interest to keep the company going. However, this can require many legal fees due to creditors' conditions.

This can often be avoided if the innovator is not in denial and moves quickly when something that will affect their business is adjusted or changed. Yes, changing things in a business can be uncomfortable—but ending up with no business and having to close the doors is much worse.

This writer knows a businessman who went through this many years ago in his father's family business. The father refused to accept it and fell into denial, even though the writing was on the wall that the business was facing some very serious problems. So, the days of bankruptcy court arrived shortly thereafter. It was not pretty. Instead of ending up in reorganization, the vendors were so upset, feeling that the father did not care for them, that they argued to the court that the current business should not be allowed to continue because of its current mismanagement. Well, this is exactly what the court decided. It sided with the creditors and ordered that the keys to the business be immediately handed over to the landlord's representative. The landlord ended up with a running business in his hands.

By this time, the son was exhausted with warning his father that there were many problems that needed addressing. However, the father continued to be in denial. The writer will never forget the look on the son's face when he was telling the story and having to recount the whole painful experience. As tears rolled down his cheeks, he made a comment that the writer will never forget. "That was the most humbling and sad day of my life," he said. "I felt like something had died inside of me as I handed the keys to the landlord's representative".

So, the next time you feel like denial is the best approach to take, think again!

WISDOM

The word wisdom is defined as "the quality of having experience, knowledge, and good judgement, the quality of being wise".

Wisdom can help us gain health, money, and other possessions. There is no doubt that wisdom is a virtue!

In business, wisdom must be a possession that is embedded into the innovator. As the innovator attempts to achieve something that no one has yet, there is no doubt that experience and knowledge must be applied.

Innovators are usually very knowledgeable within their specific industries, and most of the time when they are attempting to innovate, they use their vast experience and knowledge to improve existing product or services. Sometimes they may be attempting to innovate a truly revolutionary game changer or disrupter and this most definitely takes wisdom.

There was a king from history called king Solomon. Solomon was a young king; he knew of no conflicts with his neighbors and was a peaceful king. The Bible mentions that Solomon was favored by God, and that God asked him for whatever he wanted and said that he would grant it. Solomon asked God for wisdom, and as history shows us, he became one of the wisest, smartest, and richest men in history. You see, having wisdom will allow you to gain what you desire.

But how is wisdom gained? Well, wisdom is a gathering of experience and knowledge that is gained over time. This allows you to bank the knowledge to use when it is needed. We no doubt have experiences that others do not possess; however, we use these as reference points or learning curves and use them as a reminder of what will work and what won't.

This, no doubt, could be very useful when innovating. The innovator must always have a guide or reminder that will guide them in the right direction as they attempt to work on their innovation.

Always use the past as a learning reference to help you succeed, and never ignore the past when it comes to past experiences. Other things that can help are the experiences and stories of others about what to do—or in many cases, what not to do—when it comes to addressing innovation or growing your business.

HAMSTER WHEEL

Innovators can sometimes find themselves inside a hamster wheel. This is not only limited to their busy personal schedules. This also can many times be in a professional way.

When innovators begin to innovate, they may find themselves stuck in a rut. This may be due to them working basically on the same project, but with different added features or offerings.

It is very easy to innovate using a foundation and then to just improve on it. There's sometimes only a short window for innovating that way because of the competition; however, sometimes it's the best strategy to proceed and to stay on track before the competition can squeeze in.

However, many times it happens that innovators want to play it safe and only innovate with items or offerings that are already available. The danger with this is that the company may be limiting its future by narrowing its offering. This is done by working on the same things, but with a different spin. The so-called spin may come from added features or innovations that are created from current products or services. Naturally there is always a need to refresh current products or service offerings, and this is highly encouraged, especially when it's the company's bread and butter offering.

The smartest strategy, though, is to look for innovations that will work to expand your offerings. This will give the company a good reputation in the industry and will ensure that employee morale remains at a very high level.

Employees may sometimes get an idea that the innovations that the company is working on are just the same old things, with nothing substantially new to offer. However, if this appears to be the case, the leader of the company must be a good communicator and must be able to explain in detail the company's current strategy and where it will lead in the future.

If this is what the company needs to do to survive, then it must be conveyed to all the employees so that they do not get the incorrect impression that the company is stuck on the proverbial hamster wheel. Employees must all be assured that eventually the company will begin to expand its innovations, and this will ultimately continue to spur interest and continued growth in the company.

BEWARE OF THE JACKAL

The jackal is a lonely animal; it prays at night and usually eats the leftovers of other animals. It usually only hunts by itself or in a couple.

Jackals are very cunning animals and will do anything for an easy meal. In the business world, this type of individual preys off others, always posing as an honest businessperson. They always bring a proposal or business idea and promise the world if they are just given just a chance.

If the opportunity that they seek is given to them, they sometimes see it as an opportunity for a sure and easy kill, and they may attempt to take the company over with one fell swoop.

When dealing with jackals, you must be clear and concise and make sure that any agreement is written and detailed enough to avoid any opportunity for spin or confusion. The agreement should contain a definitive time period that it will be good for. Not having a detailed agreement before entering into a deal with a jackal may result in chaos or lawsuits.

Jackals are infamous for promising grandiose things but will always fall short. This is due to their knowledge beforehand that the idea that they propose will simply not work because they have already failed at it—yet they will never disclose this important fact.

Jackals will always make an offering very juicy and will assure prosperity for anyone accepting it. They move from merchant to merchant trying to get a deal until they find someone that will do it with them.

Jackals are very resourceful animals that can easily adjust to the terrain or conditions, the same way there are individuals who, even when their proposal doesn't work, will attempt to gain knowledge from others—and many times will gain some of your company's intelligence to begin developing their own new innovation and to top it off with your money.

If you allow this to take place, you will be in for a rude awakening, for this jackal will go solo with his successful innovation and never share your fair share of the success. The writer has seen how this happens and is writing about it as a warning to you. Always be vigilant and aware if this type of individual appears around you.

Your long journey to success will mean that you must take on predators that are very cunning. Do not fall prey to them, for they will leave you hurt and possibly ruined.

GREED

In business, greed is very prevalent. There are movies in today's modern society that glorify greed even as having lines like "greed is good."

This writer is not going to judge individuals about whether they are greedy or not, as this is for everyone to personally answer themselves. The main question is, can greed be good? All the past societies over the history of mankind that were built on a greedy foundation gradually faded and died.

A society that comes to mind is the Roman Empire. For many centuries, the Romans were the greatest world power that the world had ever seen. But as Roman societies' morality began to erode, so did the empire. Many history books mention the vast Coliseum and arenas that were built to give the citizens a form of entertainment that was called games. These were a fight to the death of man against man or man against beast.

These games were bloody events, with the spectators screaming for more, never being able to get enough.

However, the games were not the only depravities that the Roman society engaged in, they were also famous for practicing gluttony. This is a condition where a person eats and drinks until they cannot consume any longer due to being completely full, so they make themselves throw up and as soon as that is done with, the process of consuming proceeds many times over.

Slavery was also practiced by the Romans and freedom of worship did not exist. There was also the practice of prostitution that was well accepted, as well. This is all part of displaying greed.

The definition for the word greed is "an intense and selfish desire for something, especially wealth, power, or food."

So, given those facts, we should never think that greed can help us be successful for the long term. Innovators would be wise to stay away from displaying any sign of greed and should strive to be well-balanced individuals. This will ensure that you will be observed as a balanced person and a steady leader, and your team will always continue to follow you.

Greed can make an innovator reach out too far and to take risks that they do not have to take. If greed pushes us to take added risk, then it can surely destroy us. Just like you would stay away from predators in the jungle, stay away from greed.

HONESTY

While on your journey to success, the road will be full of temptation. This may come in the form of wanting to take shortcuts in one way or another, usually for material gain. Many forms of temptation appear or are offered by others in the form of cash.

In business, this is one of the most common methods of being dishonest. The practice of accepting cash for an exchange of information, or for any other reason, is also being dishonest.

Individuals that deal in dishonest ways hurt people and hurt the whole company, for the information that may be handed off to the competition will be used to hurt the company, its employees and their families and this will damage many other by standards.

The word honesty has to do with being a respected and honorable individual. The societies that are built on those types of principles have become world powers. It is quite evident that using these principles—which mean being honest—will help any innovator who is trying to build their team.

A successful team that is successful for the long term will surely be built on a foundation of honesty, mutual respect and being truthful.

What makes it difficult for innovators to stay honest is the long lag that it takes to succeed when innovating and, at the same time, having to deal with their day to day financial needs.

One way that an innovator can alleviate economic pressure while innovating is by selling stock and getting investors. However, the process of securing this type of funding also requires a high degree of honesty. "Disclosure" is a very commonly used word and is even required by law when negotiating those type of transactions. The importance of honesty, and full disclosure and transparency, is to protect investors' money. Investors often invest their retirements or their home equities, which are assets that take a long time to create. Many times, the investor has been saving the money for the future well-being and education of future generations for many years.

Securing and handling those type of funds needs to be exercised with much care and responsibility. The need to represent investors' money is so important that innovators must take care of those type of assets even more so than they take care of their own money. Once an innovator becomes successful in making a good return for their investors, the innovator's reputation will sky-rocket, and securing further funding will not be a problem.

THE FINISH LINE TOWARDS
YOUR JOURNEY TO SUCCESS

After reading this book, you may find out that you are not willing to sacrifice yourself through this type of journey, and I salute you for this, for it is better to wait and get prepared than to proceed. It is also better to come to the realization inside of whether you do or do not feel it, that this is not for you. However, this writer feels that most of you will embark on your journey to success as soon as possible—or are now at this very time already confronting many of the situations that we have discussed in going on your journey.

The writer's motivation for writing this book—you can call it an innovator's aid—is to encourage innovators and entrepreneurs alike to follow their dreams so that they can benefit from the hard work once it is accomplished. The innovator must always be aware that success will not be gained on the first attempt and should always be prepared to continue and press ahead even if it takes several more attempts to reach the finish line to the journey to success.

Again, as a reminder, your journey to success is no different than a journey through the jungle. It can be easily compared and is equally as dangerous. Going through the innovation process, it is very easy to become ensnared and paralyzed with fear. The jungle is full of cannibals and predatory wild animals, is snake infested, the rivers are crawling with crocodiles and swarming with hungry piranhas. There may also be other human factions trying to hunt you down at the same time.

Now, the writer knows that this is a lot to process while going through the plans for your journey. What makes it even more difficult is that you will be attempting to do something that more than likely you have never attempted before.

The cannibals represent the greedy competitors that will want to eat your innovation as soon as it is introduced into the marketplace. The predators can come in forms of vendors, customers, naysayers, etc. The snakes may be people who are insiders in your business and who will sell your secret information for quick cash. The piranhas may come in the form of employees who are difficult, and who—if left unchecked—can create a negative frenzy that will have the potential of taking down your business by carving it from the inside out.

As you confront some of these situations during your journey to success, you will learn from these experiences. Make sure to memorize every one of them as valuable experiences, for this is the way that wisdom is gained. Once you reach the finish line of the road of success, you will feel the excitement and ecstasy of victory, for at this point it is more than likely you have gained success, as you have worked hard and endured many challenges during your journey. You have arrived. Now go out there and carve out your piece of success—and don't forget, when you reach success, to help the world become a better place.

Congratulations,
and Welcome to an Elite Group!
EPILOGUE

Innovators come from all different walks of life. Some are young, others are older. Many come from other parts of the world to open businesses here in the United States, as our enterprise system allows free competition and allows anyone wanting to get into business to just go ahead and do so.

Whether you come from a different part of the world or not does not matter. The rich part about the United States is that, with its great diversity, it constantly creates endless dynamic possibilities of different ideas, and views, tastes, preferences, etc.

If you were born and raised in the United States you have been very fortunate to live here, learn the language, and to have gotten educated here as well.

This country is truly a beacon of democracy, freedom, business, and free enterprise for the rest of the world. It allows anyone to try their hand at building a business if that's what they desire.

So welcome to the playground of enterprise and innovation! Give it your best and continue to use this guide as a reference point and road map for wherever you want to go to during your journey to success.

This guide comes packed with useful information. These experiences have been dedicated and compiled while building not only successful innovations and inventions that have sold millions of dollars of goods, but also successful business models from the ground up. To this day, these businesses continue to succeed within their industry and hold a substantial part of the market share within their product space.

This guide is full of real business stories and experiences. It has worked as a map to build multiple successful businesses and continues to be a reminder and constant guiding light on a going forward and long-term basis. So do not forget to constantly refer to it; it will make your job of building a business and being an innovator much easier. It will also help in keeping balance throughout your building years far into the future.